Rage Against the Dying

Elizabeth Sigmund

Rage Against the Dying

**Campaign Against
Chemical and Biological Warfare**

Pluto  Press

First published 1980 by Pluto Press Limited
Unit 10, Spencer Court, 7 Chalcot Road, London NW1 8LH

Copyright © Elizabeth Sigmund 1980
ISBN 0 86104 091 0 paperback

Cover designed by Graeme Murdoch

Photoset by Photobooks (Bristol) Limited,
28/30 Midland Road, St Philips, Bristol
Printed in Great Britain by
REDWOOD BURN LIMITED
Trowbridge & Esher

Contents

Preface/7
1. The Evidence/*9*
2. Nerve Gas/*18*
3. Nancekuke/*28*
4. CS Gas/*43*
5. Research and Experiments/*58*
6. Hazards/*76*
7. Official Policy and Public Protest/*85*
8. Open Day at Nancekuke/*96*
9. Implications of CBW/*103*
   Bibliography/115
   Index/117

Geneva Protocol

Whereas the use in war of asphyxiating, poisonous or other gases, and of all analogous liquids, materials or devices, has been justly condemned by the general opinion of the civilised world . . . to the end that this prohibition shall be universally accepted as a part of International Law, binding alike the conscience and practice of nations;
 DECLARE:
 That the High Contracting Parties . . . accept this prohibition, agree to extend this prohibition to the use of bacteriological methods of warfare and agree to be bound by . . . this declaration.
 The High Contracting Parties will exert every effort to induce other States to accede to the present Protocol.
 17 June 1925

UN General Assembly Resolution 2162B (XX1):
. . . calls for strict observance by all states of the Geneva Protocol of 1925.

 5 December 1966

Preface

In 1967, when I was thirty-nine years old, I heard about a Ministry of Defence research establishment at Porton Down, which was working on chemical and biological warfare. CBW.

How those three letters were to change my life. In March of that year the BBC broadcast a radio programme called 'Make a Desolation and Call it Peace' based on an international conference on CBW held in London and organised by the Bernal Peace Library. What emerged clearly from the programme was the need for a grass-roots movement. To this end I wrote to *The Observer* in April 1968:

> Would any reader interested in an attempt to press the government to consider unilateral renunciation of the research and stockpiling of chemical and biological weapons contact me, with the object of assessing the amount of concern among responsible people on this subject.
> This is a non-political attempt and if the response is encouraging it could form the basis for a country-wide petition.

Clumsy, but effective. During the following weeks answers poured in.

Innumerable copies of a suitably-worded petition were sent over a two-year period to Denis Healey as Minister of Defence but no acknowledgement was ever received. By now the press was becoming really interested and I was constantly asked to ring the national papers with any information I obtained. Much of the information coming to light was news to journalists as well as to politicians, and even to members of the Cabinet.

In 1968 students at Exeter University discovered that there was a Ministry of Defence grant at that time for work on ricin – a highly toxic substance – in the chemistry department. As a result a teach-in on CBW was arranged.

After the teach-in, I was invited to Plymouth to appear on television, and in May 1968 to London to meet a group of people from various peace organisations to form an anti-CBW group. The meeting was televised and reported in several national papers. I realised that people *did* care, that we *could* become a voice for an otherwise unrepresented section of society. There was no turning back.

Much later it was suggested that I try to write the history of this campaign and, thanks to the Joseph Rowntree Charitable Trust in York, I was awarded a small grant for the purpose.

The book could not have been written without the loving patience and support of my family and friends, in particular my husband Bill, who has done all the typing, and Hepzibah Menuhin and Tom and Eileen Griffiths; and without the practical advice which has come from those journalists and scientists who believe that this book *must* be written.

All the mistakes are my own; all the virtues have been lent to me.

1

The Evidence

In June 1968 the BBC showed a documentary film on CBW called 'A Plague on Your Children'. It was made for the *Horizon* series by Adrian Malone and Dominic Flessati.

On 5 June, the day before it was due to be screened, *The Sun* newspaper carried a front page headline: 'BBC fears ban on germ warfare film'. The article alleged that the Ministry of Defence was concerned because certain of the Swedish sequences in the film showed experiments with nerve gas, a biological weapon and a dog suffering from the effects of a psychochemical. The only scenes the Ministry of Defence allowed to be shot at Porton were of experiments with a tear gas (CS), carried out on mice and rats fastened in ranks of metal boxes. Whether the BBC seriously considered such a ban is not known, but the story certainly guaranteed interest in the programme.

The film was made largely in America and Sweden, as the USA was pleased and proud of its CBW expertise, while the Swedish government has a more open attitude to its CBW research which is carried out jointly by the Ministries of Health and Defence. A high proportion of their research is open to scrutiny and much of it is genuinely geared to the protection of the population by producing antidotes where possible, designing detection systems and providing gas masks, protective clothing and gas-proof cribs for babies, as well as atomic, chemical and biological shelters for civilians.

The contrast in the film between the Swedish defensive posture, the American interest in super weapons and Britain's almost total secrecy was most striking.

The facts which emerged from the film were that certain

substances were already tested, approved and stockpiled in the armoury of viable weapons, in Russia and America at least.

The Swedish experiment showing the speed and effectiveness of nerve gas as a killer made it an obvious number one weapon. The subject was a rabbit, and one tiny drop of nerve gas put onto its skin produced convulsions, gasping, asphyxiation and death within minutes. We were told that the first form of nerve gas was developed by the Germans shortly before the second world war as an offshoot of research. It was called tabun, and much of the initial testing was believed to have been carried out in the Nazi concentration camps. It was never used in war, but when the German production plant was captured the Russians and Americans took over the research and produced sarin, which is more toxic, and later Britain and America developed even more effective forms called the V agents. They were developed at Porton in Britain, and at Edgewood Arsenal, Maryland, in the United States.

The other substances ('agents' as they are known in CBW jargon) mentioned in the film fall roughly into three categories: biological weapons, harassing agents and incapacitators.

Under the first heading came bubonic plague, pulmonary anthrax, botulism, encephalitis and cholera, to mention just a few. The harassing agents were DM, CN and CS. They are tear gases, and are also called lachrymators. Lastly, the incapacitators discussed in the programme were the psychochemicals BZ, LSD, DMT and STP.

Bubonic plague and the other diseases cited are already encountered in the natural environment, but the concept of deliberate infection in war adds a different dimension.

We were shown anthrax spores being harvested from culture tanks by suction equipment and stored in rows of drums, and told that Britain had conducted an experiment in the second world war on an island called Gruinard off the coast of Scotland. This island was used to test bombs and cannon shells loaded with anthrax spores, and the experiment was so effective that Gruinard has been made unapproachable for a minimum of one hundred years.

The tear gases sound reasonably mild, though in fact they are extremely unpleasant substances. CS was developed at Porton in the mid-1950s to replace CN and DM which were considered too toxic, so much so that DM at least might have been held to contravene the Geneva protocol. However CS is still far from mild in its effects and causes extreme pain in the eyes, nose and throat, profuse tears and salivation, constriction of the chest and difficulty in breathing, vomiting and diarrhoea and, in humid conditions, it can cause severe burns.

The psychochemicals are bizarre weapons indeed, intended to cause temporary mental derangement and panic. The BBC film showed a beagle, after being given atropine, in a state of total disorientation, trying to climb the walls of a circular metal chamber, and later showed several American servicemen suffering from the effects of BZ, who were trying to walk straight, climb fences and answer questions; they appeared to be completely lost to reality.

This is only a very small selection of the possible chemical and biological agents which are listed as viable weapons, that is, on which full research and testing programmes have been carried out along with the development of suitable delivery systems.

The testing of such substances on humans is a controversial subject about which the Ministry of Defence is extremely reticent. However, in the course of the film Eric Haddon, ex-Director of Porton Chemical Defence Experimental Establishment (CDEE), had this to say about CS gas: 'We have no evidence whatever that this agent is lethal. It has been tested against aged people, asthmatic people, young people, etc.' Where does one find aged and asthmatic people on whom to test this extremely unpleasant gas?

An interview with General Rothschild (US army, retired) in the film was also most disquieting. He described nerve gas as 'clean kill', praising its effectiveness against cities and valuable installations which might be of use to the occupying power, as it flushes out and kills the people, leaving the buildings and plant undamaged. This means that it is a far more useful and viable weapon for any power than the totally destructive and long lasting effects of nuclear weapons.

General Rothschild described how two or three planes spraying a city with a fine aerosol of nerve gas and could kill up to ninety per cent of the population, and leave the rest seriously damaged.

As he graphically described it, the health authorities could not possibly cope with any of this. He showed too how one ship or submarine with spraying equipment could sail down the west coast of Britain, using the strong prevailing west wind to disseminate a cloud of germs over a large area of this country.

The press reaction to 'A Plague on Your Children' was tremendous; every leading paper and tabloid, and many of the specialist journals, gave space to it. *The Sun* had a double-page spread of outrage: 'War by Plague. The Poor Man's Hydrogen Bomb'.

The next piece of documentary evidence gathered was a thesis written by two students from Newcastle University, Judith Nottingham and John Cookson. It was called 'War: A New Perspective. 1968', and was an attempt to make information available to the public on this hitherto undebated subject. It was in two parts, one dealing with the admitted use of various CBW agents in the Vietnam war, and the other describing current attitudes and governmental policy in Britain and the USA.

One of the most unpleasant revelations of this thesis was the evidence – from the World Health Organisation (WHO) of the sudden and unexplained increase in the incidence of plague and cholera in Vietnam.

In two years – between 1964 and 1966 – the recorded number of plague cases increased twenty times. 2,649 cases were reported in the first six months of 1966. In fact Vietnam was the only country in South East Asia to report any cases of plague from 1958 to 1964. There were no recorded cases of cholera in South Vietnam from 1953 to 1963, but 17,221 cases were reported in the first half of 1964.

Also quoted were statements and newspaper articles from the United States about deaths from CS gas; the Americans used it in underground tunnels, bunkers and caves where Vietnamese villagers hid from the bombing. They employed blowers attached to large containers of CS gas (called Mighty Mite) to saturate such places for long periods, thus causing very high concentrations of gas. As a result of these reports, and the plant destruction programmes used by the Americans over large food producing areas of South Vietnam, there were petitions and protests organised by scientists in America, Canada and Australia. They were signed by large numbers of eminent doctors and scientists, but completely ignored by the governments concerned, and hardly mentioned in the British press.

When a motion was tabled in parliament in 1965 deploring the American use of napalm and gas in Vietnam it gained 104 signatures, but was withdrawn; and *The Times* (25 March 1965) reported Michael Stewart (then Foreign Secretary) on arrival from Washington as saying 'Britain wholly supports American action in Vietnam'.

The Newcastle thesis was a most thoroughly researched and comprehensive study of current CBW activities at that date. Judith Nottingham told me that her rooms had been burgled during the course of her research for this book, and that tapes, files and documents had been stolen. In another part of Newcastle the same thing had happened to John Cookson on the same night. It was a disturbing story and no explanation was ever given, no-one was ever caught. In 1975 I learnt from a report in *The Guardian* that a CIA man had been in Newcastle for several months at this time (1967) (Martin Walker, *The Guardian* Open File).

Also in June 1968 there came to light a most alarming piece of information. The Campaign for Nuclear Disarmament (CND) newspaper *Sanity* reported the existence of a hitherto unknown chemical warfare research station at Portreath in Cornwall, at an ex-RAF station called Nancekuke. The article was headed. 'The pictures no-one dare print' and there were aerial photographs and a plan of the buildings.

The article stated that 'one of the gases manufactured there is CS gas, which is then transported by road to the factory in Surrey where it is processed and packaged for use'. It also quoted the alleged deaths from the use of CS gas in Vietnam.

This was a bombshell, and one that had to be investigated. If Britain *was* exporting CS gas for American use in the Vietnam war, surely Britain was contravening the Geneva protocol of 1925?

In June 1968 *The Sun* reported that Vice Admiral Sir Norman Denning, secretary of the D-notice committee which governs the publication of potentially classified material, had started an investigation to decide whether the Official Secrets Act had been infringed by *Sanity* in publishing the Nancekuke photographs. In the event, no action was taken against *Sanity*, but by now the battle was raging. The accumulation of facts about CBW presented by 'A Plague on Your Children', the Newcastle thesis and the revelation of Nancekuke – all in one month – had penetrated the consciousness of Britain at last.

Pertinent questions were being asked by all the leading specialist journals and newspapers, particularly the scientific and medical journals which had been pressing for open debate on CBW for some years.

Questions asked in the House of Commons came from all quarters, but particularly from John Pardoe, Tam Dalyell and Dr David Kerr. The answers they received, however, appeared ill-informed, often totally irrelevant, and less than candid. For example, when Denis Healey was questioned by Hugh Jenkins (Labour, Putney) on 18 July 1968 about the lethality of CS gas as used in Vietnam, Healey answered:

> CS gas was first discovered in the United States [but developed in Britain] . . . and is less toxic yet more effective than tear gas. [It is a tear gas.] I find no evidence that CS as developed at Porton has been responsible for deaths in Vietnam. [This was not the question.] I had the opportunity to sniff some CS at Porton yesterday, and I am glad to say I am here today. (Laughter)

The true answer is possibly contained in an American Department of the Army Training Circular (TC-3-16) which described the use of CS flame, smoke and anti-plant agents for Vietnam. Paragraph 26 section 4 describes the use of Mighty Mite blowers for clearing caves or tunnels:

> When burning type grenades (HC smoke or CS) are used in a tunnel or other enclosed space they may cause asphyxiation to personnel in the tunnel because of oxygen depletion and carbon monoxide buildup. [A warning for the users.] A field protective gas mask will not protect against this condition. [This last in italics.]

It has been reported in the press that £250,000 worth of CS gas is exported annually by Britain, and this has never been denied.

The director of the Surrey factory, stung by reports of his firm's involvement with packaging and exporting CS gas came out with a long statement in which he denied that CS is a gas. 'It is a smoke', he said.

> If foreigners must go using the stuff improperly in confined spaces and so on, it is not our fault for helping the government to supply them . . . No discomfort is caused to our workers who handle CS. Lightheartedly we say in the factory that if you want to cure a cold spend an hour or two in the CS section.

In answer to that throwaway comment I must refer to a monograph produced by Professor Lohs for the Stockholm International Peace Research Institute (SIPRI) called 'Delayed toxic effects of CW agents' (1975, chapter 4 paragraph 4):

> There are good grounds however, for fearing that exposure to lachrymators [tear gas] can have still more serious effects. Thus Neilands, referring to results obtained by Barry, has reported the carcinogenic activity of o-chlorobenzylidene malononitrile (CS). It ought to be pointed out that the toxicological hazards of CS have often been underestimated. Attention should also be paid to the allergenic properties of CS and other riot control agents because of their obvious significance, particularly for workers and military personnel employed in production works and stores.

Yet for many years the actual chemical components of CS were classified as secret and were unknown outside the Ministry of Defence.

The anti-CBW group was invited to attend a teach-in on CBW at the House of Commons in 1968. It was addressed by specialists (such as Professor Steven Rose) and attended by a large number of MPs. I was told by one MP that 'very little is known about this area of defence by MPs, even by the Cabinet', and a member of the House of Lords, who was an MP for some time, told me that only when a Defence White Paper is published do MPs know what is going on, and then only in very broad outline, by which time the policy is a *fait accompli*.

Next came a non-move by the BBC *Tonight* programme. Thanks to *Sanity* magazine we knew of Nancekuke's existence, and that it produced CS, but little more. The producer of the programme assured me that they would do a full examination of the whole subject. Then we found out that Nancekuke had been manufacturing nerve gas and, inexplicably, when an open day was arranged for the press, the *Tonight* team was much too busy to attend.

At this time Porton's Dr Inch visited Essex University. The visit was reported in the *New Statesman*, though sadly distorted later by many papers. Tom Baistow (*New Statesman*, 17 May 1968) wrote:

> By setting up a 'free university' one thousand students and forty of the teaching staff at Colchester are directly challenging the concept, accepted by the government . . . that the sale of poison and nerve gases and worse is a normal 'defence' precaution. For some time indignation has been growing among students and dons about the implication of the research work going on in this field in British universities. At Essex their feelings came to a head last week when Dr T.A. Inch of the CDEE at Porton was invited to give a talk about toxic gases. When asked why Britain was allowing Porton's own patented CS gas, which is extremely toxic, to be made under licence to the US which is using it in Vietnam . . . Dr Inch is reported as saying 'We need the money'.

At this point a student moved beside him, saying 'Here, have some mustard gas yourself,' and sprinkled Colman's mustard powder on his sleeve. At this point there was an influx of security men and police and in the resulting chaos Dr Inch was inevitably 'jostled'.

Tom Baistow continues:

> This ended in the suspension of three students that led in turn to the setting up of the 'free university' in which the ethics of chemical and biological warfare can be openly discussed. Of course there will be the inevitable howl of 'anarchy' and 'irresponsibility' and the attempts to smear what is a deeply felt protest . . . but the truth is that in this day of constipated politics it has taken the students to think responsibly . . . one hopes that they will be able to turn it into a national debate . . . and look again at this horrific nationalised industry.

Such a debate has still not taken place, and one must be concerned at the striking difference in our own silence and secrecy when contrasted with the debate that took place in post-Watergate America. The machinery for instigating such a debate does not appear to exist in Britain, as the Official Secrets Act is used as a reason for not answering many parliamentary questions, and civil servants are not allowed to enter into any public debate.

2

Nerve Gas

There is a close chemical similarity between the organophosphorus insecticides and the nerve gases. In fact it was from information gained by Dr Gerhard Schrader during his work on organophosphorus compounds for use as insecticides in Germany before the second world war that the German military establishment became interested in these substances for use as weapons. The first form of nerve gas developed was called tabun (ethyl dimethylphosphoramidocyanidate) and was prepared by Schrader in December 1936. After this came sarin (isopropyl methyl phosphofluoridate) and later the still more toxic soman. Approximately one milligram of sarin is thought to be lethal if inhaled; death is also caused by ingestion or by skin contact. These organophosphorus compounds have a specific inhibitory action on the enzyme cholinesterase, and are thus known as anti-cholinesterases.

The transmission of nerve impulses from the brain to the muscles is passed in chemical form along the nerves. The junctions between the nerves are called synapses, and here acetylcholine is released to start the sequence which leads to muscle contraction. The muscle action is controlled by cholinesterase which breaks down the acetylcholine into its two constituent parts – acetic acid and choline – and so breaks the connection and permits the muscle to relax. If, however, the action of the cholinesterase is inhibited the muscle cannot relax, and acetyl choline builds up causing the muscle to go into a state of 'fibrillation' or spasm.

When this condition affects the whole body – as in nerve gas poisoning – all the muscles contract. Initially vision is impaired (miosis); the breathing, heart and blood pressure are affected; there is loss of control over excretion; vomiting occurs; followed by depression of the respiratory function causing asphyxiation, convulsions, coma and death.

When the war ended and the German nerve gas work was discovered, the Russian, American and British military chemists hurried home to work on improved forms of nerve gas.

Part of the war reparation given to Britain was in the form of nerve gas plant from Germany, which was set up in St Helens, Lancashire. However, as this did not seem to be a suitable area for such secret and dangerous work, it was transferred to an ex-RAF airfield called Nancekuke in Cornwall.

One of the most important results of the development of the V agents is that they broke the gas/gas mask deadlock. Soldiers or civilians attacked by a V agent would survive only if they were *completely* covered by protective clothing.

There is no doubt at all that there are facilities in the United States and Russia for the large scale production of the nerve gases, and that stockpiles now exist of nerve gases and of rockets, landmines, artillery shells, bombs and missiles for its tactical application. (WHO report on CBW, 1969.) Recently the chairperson of the Nancekuke section of the Institute of Professional and Civil Servants, John Holden, said: 'Anyone reading the newspapers and watching television news bulletins must be aware that the possibility of a chemical attack in the event of war is higher than ever before.' (*The Guardian*, 31 March 1976.)

Also, of course, protective clothing and gas masks are available for all the armed forces, including those of Britain. (Proof of this came from Jane Sully, who found an anti-CBW smock marked 'Smock/chemical and biological protective – part of suit CB Remploy 1968' on a beach called Ready Money Cove at Fowey in Cornwall on 13 October 1968. There were NATO exercises off the Cornish coast at the time and when the discovery was reported to the Fowey police, Special Branch men came and took the smock. Subsequently her small daughter was stopped by a man in a sports car and questioned about her mother, and their holiday in Hungary. This happened on two separate occasions.)

As information about nerve gas poisoning is classified, one can draw on very few sources, notably certain Swedish publications, and the work of two German professors – K. Lohs and

U. Spiegelberg – who have carried out exhaustive studies of disabled patients who had worked in the German nerve gas plants at the end of the war. Both these professors work and publish their findings openly.

However, when the Ministry of Defence quotes 'experts on nerve gas poisoning' they mean British specialists. One can but ask: where did these experts gain their experience?

The first case of alleged nerve gas poisoning in Britain came to light after the showing of Adrian Malone's film 'A Plague on Your Children' (see chapter 1, p.9). Adrian Malone received a letter, which he forwarded to me, from the wife of an ex-RAF officer, William Cockayne. The letter described the strange illness her husband had suffered since working at Porton with nerve gas in 1952. When the Cockaynes saw the film they had been struck by the story of Dr Mary Whittaker, a biochemist from King's College, London. She had described her illness and subsequent partial paralysis, the result of working with organophosphorus insecticides. After working at Cambridge for ICI she had become violently ill; she had had convulsions whenever she exerted herself, she had suffered from nausea, giddiness and severe pains in the limbs. She had been in The London Hospital for a year and had improved slowly, though physiotherapy had proved to be harmful as it had made the muscles go into spasm. She was left with paralysis of certain leg muscles. Dr Whittaker gained substantial damages from ICI when an eminent toxicologist – Dr Donald Hunter – gave evidence on her behalf in court. (This is described in his book on industrial injuries called *Health in Industry*, Penguin 1959.)

The Cockayne family was housed in a council flat in Lewisham designated 'for the use of a problem family'. Their only income was from various forms of social security. On all William Cockayne's forms he was described as an alcoholic. This was not true; he did not drink alcohol as it made him ill, and he could not afford it anyway.

He had bouts of illness and deep depression, when he lay in bed shaking, unable to move or eat for days on end; when welfare officers came to see him they reprimanded him with 'on the booze again', which seemed to form a self-perpetuating trap from which he could not escape.

Later Flt.Lt. Cockayne wrote me long letters describing the accident at Porton when his gas mask failed during trials of a weapon for firing nerve gas disc shells at a range where baboons, chimpanzees, goats, dogs, and other animals were tethered. The nerve gas was dyed red so that the extent of its dispersal was visible, and after the area appeared clear, William Cockayne went in to see what had happened to the animals, wearing full protective clothing and a gas mask. He remembered leaving the area and falling down, unable to move, and then dragging his forehead along the ground as he crawled away. He claims that he saw two other men being carried off and driven away in a jeep. He never heard anything further of them.

The next thing he remembers was coming round several weeks later in a single-bed room in a hospital. His papers said that he had last been stationed at Boscombe Down RAF station. (Boscombe Down is adjacent to Porton.) William Cockayne was discharged from the RAF while still in hospital, and diagnosed as a psychiatric case in 1954. He claims that the RAF gave him £1600, which was *not* compensation as no-one admitted that he had ever been at Porton, let alone suffered any injury there. After that he had tried to work but had had bouts of depression and loss of memory; cold weather seemed to affect him very badly, and he would become almost comatose.

He spent some of his money on going to Australia where he met and married his wife, Betty; he worked for a firm of barristers who liked and respected him, but he continued to have bouts of depression and nervous tension which lasted from six weeks to three months. He was examined by a psychotherapist in Sydney called Claire Weekes, who saw him professionally for some time.

Dr Weekes issued a report in August 1960 saying that William Cockayne appeared to suffer an annual nervous breakdown and should be freed from unnecessary stress. Dr Weekes advised him to return to Britain and to try to get help from the RAF. William Cockayne went back to England but no-one would listen to him, no-one would admit that he had ever been at Porton, and he was now designated as an alcoholic and as mentally ill. He had been an intensely loyal and ambitious RAF officer, and he could not believe that the RAF would treat anyone like this; the more desperate and angry his appeals became the more paranoic he appeared to be.

William Cockayne attempted suicide several times, and was admitted to various mental wards, but when he began talking of Porton and nerve gas he was quickly discharged again. His wife and sons were in a desperate plight, and by 1968 had descended into a state of acute poverty and despair in their Lewisham flat. Betty Cockayne begged for help from their MP, James Dickens (Labour, Lewisham) who wrote to the Minister of Defence on 26 June 1968, and asked three questions: whether Flight Lieutenant Cockayne had served at Porton; whether he had been engaged on research into nerve gases; and whether he had at any time suffered exposure to nerve gas poisoning.

On 31 July 1968, the Minister of Defence (Equipment), John Morris, replied by letter, confirming that William Cockayne had served at Porton from 1952 to 1954, that he was not engaged on research into nerve gases, but 'had taken part in field experiments to assess the vulnerability of our equipment to nerve gas weapons'. This is a curious answer, as nerve gas does not affect equipment, only living creatures.

The answer continues:

> On 5 August he was suffering from myopsis [miosis] or contraction of the pupils caused by a mild exposure to a nerve agent. He was treated for this by codeine and there was no recurrence of the complaint . . . It was not unknown for members of the Porton staff at the time to suffer mild myopsis as a result of small accidental exposure to agents. Recovery was normally complete in a few hours without any treatment at all.

Yet Davies, Holland and Rumens of the CDEE at Porton, investigating the correlation between the chemical structure and neurotoxic effect of alkyl phosphates, including DFP, sarin and derivatives, came to the following conclusion:

> The neurotoxic hazard which these substances constitute to man is a difficult problem to assess because of a) known species differences in the response to organophosphorus compounds and b) the *absence of any direct evidence* that organophosphorus compounds . . . are neurotoxic in humans . . . these have been extensively studied in the chicken . . . it must therefore be assumed that all the

organophosphorus compounds shown to be neurotoxic in chickens will under appropriate conditions produce neurotoxicity in man (Porton 1960).

This seems to be a most unsatisfactory scientific statement on which to base any claim to expertise on nerve gas poisoning in humans.

In 1969, Aldridge, Barnes and Johnson, of the New York Academy of Sciences, summed up their extensive work on delayed neurotoxicity produced by some organophosphorus compounds thus: 'It is clear that many organophosphorus compounds can produce delayed neurotoxicity in low doses.'

(These quotations were taken from the Swedish International Peace Research Institute (SIPRI) monograph 'Delayed toxic effects of chemical warfare agents', 1975.)

To return to the reply of the Minister of Defence for Equipment:

> There is no evidence that when he [Cockayne] resigned from the RAF in 1954 he made any complaints about his health having suffered from nerve gas poisoning, nor is there any evidence that he suffered any lasting ill effects from the mild dose of nerve gas he received in 1953. If you feel that an *independent medical examination*, involving as it would full access to Flight Lieutenant Cockayne's medical and service history, would be worthwhile, I would certainly have no objection. I would understand if you would prefer to have this done by a doctor unconnected with the Ministry of Defence. If you would care to suggest to Flight Lieutenant Cockayne that he should get in touch with the Ministry of Social Security they would be prepared to have him examined.

However, on 7 May 1969 James Dickens received a letter from David Ennals, the Minister for Health and Social Security, which stated:

> The consultants have now reported. The first [unnamed] who is an expert on the effects of nerve gas on man considers that it is not in the least probable that the agent to which Flight Lieutenant Cockayne was exposed had any delayed or permanent physical effect. The second consultant, who is an independent medical expert appointed by the Royal College of Physicians to advise the

Secretary of State on questions of serious doubt, found it unnecessary to examine Flight Lieutenant Cockayne as the case was so well documented. He endorses the first consultant's report.

In fact, no-one examined William Cockayne, and when James Dickens protested, he was told: 'When we go to independent consultants and ask for their opinions it is not for us to direct them in any way as to their methods of arriving at their conclusions.'

James Dickens said, in the House of Commons on 24 June 1969, that he found this reply unsatisfactory, and that it raised serious questions of principle. Indeed it did, and still does.

David Ennals rounded off his answer by saying:

> If Flight Lieutenant Cockayne or his representatives feel that medical evidence is incomplete they themselves are perfectly at liberty to obtain further evidence

knowing that there was little possibility of gaining evidence in the field of nerve gas poisoning at that time.

At this point it was obviously essential to find a truly independent source of medical knowledge on nerve gas poisoning, and to this end I wrote to Dr Julian Perry Robinson who had done a great amount of research into CBW, and who was then working with SIPRI in Stockholm. I asked him for help on this point of medical evidence, and he suggested that we get the paper by Professor U. Spiegelberg of West Germany on 'Psychopathological and neurological after-effects and permanent damage from industrial poisoning by phosphoric acid esters (alkyl phosphates)', which had been given at the 14th International Congress on Occupational Health, 1963. It described the investigations carried out on a large number of workers who were employed from 1936 to 1945 in the German war gas centres at Berlin, Spandau and Munster. 'Our researches began in 1956 and are still continuing. They include neuroradiological, electrocephalic and experimental psychological methods.'

The paper lists the neurological psychopathological delayed war poison syndromes, and describes the most common symptoms:

1. In the great majority of cases investigated we found
    a) persistent lowering of energy, with marked lack of drive
    b) lack of central nervous regulation with cephalgia, gastrointes-

tinal and cardiovascular symptoms, premature loss of sexual libido and capability
c) intolerance (to alcohol, nicotine and medicine)
d) impression of premature ageing
2. Usually we also found one or more effects of the second group of symptoms
a) depressive or subdepressive states of ill temper of a vital nature
b) cerebral central nervous (syncopal) attacks
c) slight to moderate amnestic and dementive deficiencies (predominantly microsymptoms and singular signs of extrapyramidal type).

In the next section of his paper Professor Spiegelberg mentions other reports by scientists who have published papers on delayed neurological damage, including a case frequently cited by Petry which 'showed marked psychic alterations in addition to a polyneuritic syndrome. The psychiatric after-effects from chronic exposure to insecticides published by Gershon and Shaw in 1961 are well worth noting. Critical objections to this have been raised by Barnes as well as Bidstrup.' (The latter name will assume importance later.)

The description of symptoms was an accurate picture of William Cockayne's condition.

I was able to see the science correspondents of two leading British newspapers and to give them all the evidence about William Cockayne's case, his pre-Porton background, and the Spiegelberg paper. The next day there was front page coverage of his story in both these papers, and other nationals and the local press quickly followed. *Sanity*, in September 1968, had a front page with photographs showing the shocking ageing process which had taken place in William Cockayne between 1952 and 1968 and was headed 'Britain's first nerve gas victim'.

A London correspondent of the *Sydney Morning Herald* read the Cockayne story in the British press, and was struck by (Australian) Betty Cockayne's determined struggle. The journalist rang me and, on hearing that the Cockaynes and I had never met, arranged to interview Betty Cockayne and me together.

This was my first meeting with Betty Cockayne. I had only just received and read the Spiegelberg paper, and the Cockaynes had not heard of it. Betty Cockayne told us quietly and sadly of her husband's illness, and mentioned his intolerance to medical drugs; later she said that he could not stand spirits and then mentioned to me that their married life had become very difficult because of all her husband's illness and sexual coldness. I then showed them the Spiegelberg paper, which mentions all these three symptoms; added to the other physical and psychological facts we knew, this seemed to be fairly convincing evidence.

The Australian journalist was most impressed by the story, but it was not published in Australia, either in whole or in part. We never knew why.

The Cockayne family have been helped to find a flat in Cornwall, and their lives have improved quite substantially through the kindness of friends. But no compensation was granted at that time even after a second medical tribunal had considered his case in the light of the Spiegelberg paper, and so their financial position was very difficult.

There are obviously many legal problems in such a case, mainly stemming from a lack of knowledge of nerve gas poisoning, but also compounded by the effect of the Official Secrets Act upon experts in this field. The unfortunate fact is that anyone who has access to the information and the experience necessary to become an expert has been allowed such access only *after* signing the Official Secrets Act.

Ten years later William Cockayne's son was still appealing for help for his father, and had asked David Ennals (his MP) to advise the family as to their best course of action. This appeal was, for many years fruitless.

An example of the problem of identifying the effects of nerve gas poisoning was most clearly demonstrated when it was reported that nerve gas was used in the Yemen in 1963 and again in 1967.

The first claim made by the Saudis was of six deaths 'from gas warfare' in 1963. This was never substantiated, and a UN mission which was sent to check the story 'found no evidence of the use of gas' (*New York Times*, 16 July 1963).

Later claims appear more serious, and involved United Arab Republic air raids on the villages of Kitaf on 5 January and Gahar on 10 May 1967.

On 22 March 1967 the Saudi Arabian representative to the

UN, Jamil Baroody, in a letter to U Thant, charged that UAR planes had bombed Kitaf on 5 January causing between one hundred and two hundred deaths from lethal gas. He submitted Saudi medical reports stating that victims had 'probably' been exposed to organic phosphorus compounds which reduce blood cholinesterase (UN Security News Release, S/7842, 6 April 1967).

In June 1967 the International Committee of the Red Cross (ICRC) stated that a Red Cross medical team in Yemen had 'collected various indications pointing to the use of poison gas' in the 10 May attack on Gahar. The report did not name the nation responsible for the use of gas, nor its type.

However two American columnists, Joseph Alsop and Marquis Childs, have charged unequivocally that Egypt employed nerve gas in Yemen, although they have not revealed their sources.

Another charge appeared on 9 June 1967 in *The Reporter* from 'a top secret US Intelligence Report' that in two raids on 13 and 14 May on the towns of Najran and Jizan the Egyptians dropped canisters containing a highly sophisticated poison gas that attacks the nervous system and is fatal in very small quantities.

The evidence which emerges is inconclusive. But in a report by Andre Rochat, head of the ICRC delegation to Yemen in 1967, published in the American magazine *Scientist and Citizen* (August 1967) he concludes: 'Clearly lethal poison gas . . . has been used in Yemen. Whether the more recently developed nerve gases, never before used in war, have been introduced in an attack on Yemeni civilians is a question that remains unresolved by the publicly available evidence.'

3

Nancekuke

After the disclosure that a chemical defence research establishment existed at Nancekuke in Cornwall, a flood of requests for information came from newspapers and MPs. I immediately made an appointment to meet Gwyneth Dunwoody, Labour MP for Exeter, at her surgery in Exeter; her husband, Dr John Dunwoody, was Labour MP for Camborne and I felt that she might be concerned and helpful. I was wrong – her attitude seemed to me to be one of bored condescension. She more or less assured me that the whole thing was an hysterical storm in a teacup, and that nothing untoward was going on at Nancekuke.

However, when I left her office, a diminutive west country man ran after me and said: 'Don't let on that I've said a word, but many of us are worried about that place. Don't give up asking questions and in particular ask about the undersea pipeline which cost a million pounds to construct.' He was obviously nervous and spoke in a fast whisper.

The majority of the local west country press appeared to wish to minimise the effect of Nancekuke's existence in order to protect the tourist industry. However, the *Plymouth Independent* took a very firm line from the beginning, and stated its deep concern for the safety of the population of Cornwall, and in particular for the health of the Nancekuke employees.

In August 1969, Thomas Griffiths, who had worked at Nancekuke as a toxic fitter since the early 1950s, contacted Bill Cockayne (see chapter 2) telling him of his own illness. As Thomas Griffiths had signed the Official Secrets Act when he was employed by the Ministry of Defence he was extremely frightened of disclosing any details of the substances with which he worked, or the type of work it was. Thomas Griffiths related, when we met, the story of his work (in very bare outline) and the illness which he had suffered since working at Nancekuke. All the employees at Nancekuke had carried printed cards which stated: 'In the event of symptoms developing contact the Medical Officer of Health, Nancekuke' with a telephone number. The 'symptoms' mentioned had never been explained to them, except as 'contraction of the pupils of the eyes and constriction of the chest'. He told me that everyone had daily blood tests, but did not know why. (We now know that they were to test the blood cholinesterase levels.) His family had no idea what Nancekuke was nor what his work entailed.

Tom Griffiths suffers syncopal attacks and muscle spasms; he has been told that the constriction and pain he suffers in his chest are the result of a heart condition, though he has had no medication for it.

In 1964 he reported that the pains in his chest were causing him some discomfort; nevertheless he continued to work for two weeks. Later he was informed that he had suffered a heart attack over this period, and was put into hospital for tests. He was off work for six months, and then did light work until early in 1969.

In November 1970 he went to the Royal Devon and Exeter Hospital and was examined by Dr. D.B. Shaw who reported that Tom did not have angina, nor could he detect any heart damage. Dr Shaw wrote: 'I would not consider that his present symptom of exhaustion was a form of angina, nor would I consider it to be cardiac in origin.' (11 November 1970.)

Tom Griffiths's attacks, with complete loss of consciousness, are preceded by a feeling of panic, giddiness, tension and intense heat. If he is indoors he rushes out into the air, and removes some of his clothes. Even in icy conditions he is drenched with sweat. Such attacks are followed by a long period of complete exhaustion and debility when he finds it hard to move even a hand. He suffers permanent weakness and cold in his legs. He also has pain and tension in his neck, head and chest, and his eyesight is variable. His memory is very poor and he has to make a tape recording of anything he wishes to remember.

He cannot tolerate normal medication or alcohol, and his GP finds this aspect of the case very puzzling. If his wife uses an aerosol, such as a hairspray or deodorant, and Tom comes into the room he immediately begins to cough and fight for breath. He has frequent nightmares. I was convinced that his symptoms were akin to those suffered by Bill Cockayne and Dr Mary Whittaker.

I wrote to Dr John Dunwoody (then MP for Camborne, the constituency in which Nancekuke is situated), Peter Bessel, who was interested in Bill Cockayne's case and John Pardoe, MP for North Cornwall, who was also most concerned about Nancekuke.

Dr Dunwoody was neither interested nor convinced that there was any connection between their illnesses and Nancekuke, but John Pardoe took up the cudgels and asked the Secretary of State for Defence to investigate the incidence of death and disability among persons who had been employed at Nancekuke. John Morris, Minister of Defence (Equipment) stated in a written reply: 'It would be wrong to assume that service at Nancekuke had anything to do with the cases reported in the press.' He did, however, undertake to look into any particular case which Mr Pardoe felt required investigation.

In another reply John Morris stated: 'So far as can be traced there have been only two cases in the history of the CDE Nancekuke of persons employed there claiming that they have suffered from nerve gas poisoning.'

On the same day Ivor Richard, Defence Under-Secretary for the army, said that the Ministry refused to carry out a general investigation, and strenuously denied that the Official Secrets Act would prevent persons from telling their family or doctor about the nature of their work.

> Contrary to some reports it is just not true that the Official Secrets Act or any other security regulation prevents a National Health doctor from obtaining information from Nancekuke about the substances their patients have been working with. However, each employee carries a card advising his doctor how to get this information from the doctor at Nancekuke.

No information about the substances was ever given to any doctor treating Tom Griffiths or by anyone connected with Nancekuke or the Ministry of Defence, until the Department of Health and Social Security tribunal which was set up in 1969. Tom has letters from the Ministry of Defence 'specifically forbidding him to discuss any aspect of his work at Nancekuke, under the rules of the Official Secrets Act.

In December 1969 John Pardoe gained assurances from the Ministry of Defence and the Department of Health and Social Security that independent tribunals would be set up to examine all cases of alleged illness resulting from work at Nancekuke and, in cases of death, relatives would be allowed to lodge a claim. The Ministry of Defence, through John Morris, assured John Pardoe that all the evidence would be made available to the tribunals. He also said: 'There is no evidence whatsoever that a sub-lethal dose of nerve gas has any long term effects.' The Ministry had tried to reproduce these effects in animals and 'the results had been negative'.

The fact is that at this time there was a long list of publications – American, British and German – on cholinesterase inhibitors. In a paper called 'Anticholinesterases – paralysis in man following poisoning by cholinesterase inhibitors' (Dr Patricia Lesley Bidstrup, *Chemistry in Industry*, 12 June 1954) the author wrote: 'The use of organic phosphorus compounds as insecticides has resulted in many cases of acute poisoning. The symptoms, signs and treatment of acute poisoning by these compounds, being well known, will not be discussed in this paper.' Dr Bidstrup then described the history of accidents with cholinesterase inhibitors going back to 1899. TOCP (triorthocresyl phosphate) caused the first known cases, which were reported by Lorot in 1899.

Hunter, Perry and Evans in 1944 had reported three cases of polyneuritis in men manufacturing TOCP. Zeligs followed up 316 patients admitted to Cincinnatti general hospital in 1930 after drinking a beverage called Jamaican Ginger which contained about two per cent of TOCP; they suffered paralysis and six years later sixty of them were still in institutions.

Dr Bidstrup then described a man admitted to The London Hospital on 26 January 1950, who had been working for six months in a chemical factory 'as a process worker on the manufacture of the meta and para isomers of tricresyl phosphate for use as plasticisers . . . the final product contained less than one per cent of TOCP'. She then outlined the by now familiar symptoms.

On '10 March 1951 he was discharged from hospital. The patient is likely to remain permanently and almost totally disabled.'

Dr Bidstrup's paragraph is of crucial importance.

> Because we were not aware of the work of Bloch and Hottinger (1943) when this patient first became ill, cholinesterase activity was not estimated until September 1951, by which time it was within normal limits for both plasma and the red cell enzyme.

In a period of 20 months the patients' cholinesterase level had returned to normal – yet he was permanently disabled. The importance of this will be made clear when we later consider the findings of the medical tribunal on Tom Griffiths in 1975.

(Dr Bidstrup also reported the cases of three people who in August 1951 developed the symptoms and signs of acute organic phosphorus poisoning.)

Tom Griffiths was a toxic fitter doing maintenance work in a storage cubicle at Nancekuke with another fitter on 31 March 1958. They had been told by a scientific officer that the cubicle was 'clean' and that no protective clothing or gas masks were needed. When Tom noticed a drop of liquid hanging from a pipe above their heads he knew that it was sarin GB, and that there was a leak. He and his friend got out of the cubicle, but their eyesight was affected, their blood cholinesterase levels dropped and they were kept under observation at work for three weeks. No treatment was given. Tom's cholinesterase level had dropped from 133 to 105, and did not return to normal until June 1959, a period of fifteen months. Here Dr Bidstrup's paper is valuable:

> We would like to emphasise that atropine, which counteracts the muscarinic and central nervous system effects of inhibition of cholinesterase is not an antidote to the nicotinic effects, and that no antidote to these effects is known at the present time. We have observed that the hypotonia of voluntary muscle which is one of the nicotinic effects of acute organic phosphorus poisoning, persists far longer than is generally realised.

Tom was not treated with atropine, or anything else.

(In February 1979, Dr Mary Whittaker told me that, in her opinion, Tom would not have suffered such prolonged and severe symptoms if he had had proper treatment. She said that it was so lucky for her that she had had 'a saint, Donald Hunter' to treat her and then fight for compensation.)

Tom Griffiths was now able to do only very restricted work. At this time neither his wife nor doctor knew that Tom had been working with nerve gas.

The workmate who was exposed at the same time as Tom was killed in a road accident.

Tom's symptoms led his doctor to suspect angina as there was evidence of cardiovascular distress, and in 1964 Tom Griffiths suffered a mild coronary thrombosis, of which he was not aware for some months. (The Spiegelberg paper mentions cardiovascular symptoms, among others that Tom suffered.)

When news of Nancekuke's real function came to light in 1969 Tom Griffiths's doctor was told for the first time that nerve gas was being manufactured there and that Tom's work as a toxic fitter brought him into direct contact with it. He learned also of the accident which caused Tom's cholinesterase level to drop so sharply, and stay down for at least fifteen months. He referred Tom to a consultant neurologist at Truro, Dr A.B. Herring, who said that it was likely that nerve gas was responsible for his prolonged history of weakness, muscle twitching and various neurological and psychological irregularities. Tom's GP then certified him as unfit for work because of sarin GB poisoning.

At this point Dr Donald Hunter, then of Guy's Hospital, London, and a leading expert in industrial toxicology, examined Tom Griffiths and gave his opinion that 'the balance of probability is that sarin GB poisoning is responsible'. He later said that he was 'convinced' that this was the case.

In 1971 this report, with five other medical opinions supporting Dr Hunter's findings, went before a Department of Health medical board, who advised an interim disability award. However the Department of Health in London had also had the case history assessed by an expert in anti-cholinesterase poisoning – Dr Patricia Bidstrup. She disagreed with all six doctors, adding, however, 'I have not had the advantage of examining the patient'.

On the basis of her report Sir Keith Joseph, Secretary of State for Health at this time, appealed against the board's findings.

Pending this appeal a second medical board examined Tom

Griffiths in 1972, and recommended a second interim payment. Again Sir Keith Joseph appealed on the basis of Dr Bidstrup's 1971 report, and in 1974 a third medical board found that:

> Griffiths's loss of faculty resulted from the anti-cholinesterase action of organic phosphorus compounds

and recommended a once and for all payment of £467. They stated that the condition was 'valid for life' and set a 'ten per cent degree of disability.'

The Health Secretary was now Barbara Castle, who also appealed against payment, citing Dr Bidstrup's original opinion, though Dr Bidstrup still had not met nor examined Tom Griffiths.

Between 1970 and 1974 the solicitors acting for the Amalgamated Union of Engineering Workers (AUEW) on behalf of Tom Griffiths, were preparing to institute a high court action against the Ministry of Defence to prove negligence. They had all the evidence of the previous medical boards, consultants' findings, expert scientific literature on long term damage from exposure to nerve gas, and all Tom's papers and correspondence relating to the case.

The solicitors had Tom examined by a Dr Kocen, and on the strength of his report said that, although all the medical evidence was not consistent, they felt that the symptoms and disability were not due to exposure to nerve gas.

Dr Hunter reaffirmed his conviction that Tom Griffiths was suffering the long-term effects of exposure to sarin GB but, when asked to give evidence in court on Tom's behalf, wrote to the solicitors on 26 October 1970:

> Has it occurred to you that the reluctance of [another doctor] and myself to provide you with details . . . is connected with violation of the Official Secrets Act? Obliquely we have been threatened with this.

Despite this letter from Dr Hunter, the solicitors answered a letter of mine in 1975 which asked why they had abandoned the case against the Ministry of Defence, saying that the Official Secrets Act had 'no bearing on this case whatsoever'. This idea is repeated by the Ombudsman who reported on the whole issue in August

1978, although he had had no contact with the solicitors during his investigation.

The terms in which the Ombudsman reports the permission given by the Ministry of Defence are important.

> There will be no objection to your client or to witnesses disclosing to you and your client's medical advisers evidence as to the substances handled by your client . . . and the type of plant used . . . and the work your client was doing.

This minimal clearance led the Ombudsman to conclude that he found no evidence that the Official Secrets Act had been improperly used to hinder Mr Griffiths's case.

But the central issue at stake is that expert medical opinion in the field of long-term damage resulting from exposure to organic phosphorus compounds has to be substantiated in open court. The doctor would therefore need to discuss research results. To quote the observed effects on chickens (as Porton had done) would not be considered sufficient in a court of law.

Any such research is highly sensitive, and most certainly covered by the Official Secrets Act. Apparently, to quote the findings of Professor Spiegelberg and even Dr Bidstrup herself has not proved persuasive enough for successive tribunals and so would not produce the desired result in a high court case against the Ministry of Defence, especially as Dr Hunter states that he was hampered by threats of the consequences of any 'violation', however oblique.

Professor Spiegelberg was a vital link in this chain. He offered to come and undertake a long detailed clinical examination in preparation for giving evidence in court. The offer was not taken up.

Eventually the solicitors advised Tom not to continue with the case as 'further action cannot lead to success'. The solicitors tell me that the union notified them that it would not continue to support the action.

The solicitors wrote to Tom Griffiths advising him and telling him that, if he still wanted to pursue the action he should 'seek the services of another solicitor without delay'. That would mean that the union would not be standing the costs of course.

In 1975, despite Dr Bidstrup's protestations that she might not be accepted as an objective, unbiased and independent person, the Department of Health insisted that she examine Tom Griffiths. Not surprisingly, the examination resulted in the confirmation of her earlier verdict: 'None of these conditions is in any way related to the episode of mild sarin GB poisoning.'

The report of the 1975 medical tribunal on Tom Griffiths, held at Plymouth by Patrick Brannigan QC as chairperson, and consisting of C.T. Andrews and C. Bruce Perry – one a consultant physician and the other a professor of medicine – studied reports on Tom and various publications including Spiegelberg's paper and 'Delayed toxic effects of chemical warfare agents' published by SIPRI. The report by Dr Kocen of 15 January 1974 for the solicitors was submitted by Tom Griffiths, who was present with his wife, but unrepresented by a medical or legal adviser.

The report states: 'The medical tribunal found Mr Griffiths's physical condition excellent.' Tom's GP says that he finds this sentence unbelievable. 'No doctor could possibly claim that of Tom.' At the same time they found Bidstrup's reports of January 1971 and 11 August 1975 accurate.

The tribunal agreed that he was exposed to 'mild organo-phosphorus poisoning on 31 March 1958' but that 'cholinesterase level returned to normal within a short time'. Later in the same report they say 'the cholinesterase level returned to normal by April 1959', thirteen months later. The GP told the tribunal that it had not returned to normal until June 1959. Fifteen months. In Dr Bidstrup's own paper the anonymous patient whose cholinesterase level was normal twenty months after exposure is 'permanently and almost totally disabled'.

However by 1975 Dr Bidstrup said of Tom: 'his subsequent symptoms of shortness of breath, lack of energy and anxiety with depression could be and are (sic) related to the myocardial ischaemia and coronary thrombosis of 1964'.

Dr Kocen finds that Mr Griffiths's vasomotor instability causes his syncopal attacks and that all are attributable to ischaemic disease which in turn are accounted for by cervical spondylosis (arthritis of the bones of the neck). As Tom Griffiths says, the tribunal agreed his symptoms come from

a) a mild thrombosis in 1964 – Dr Bidstrup
b) cervical spondylosis – Dr Kocen

Are the two synonymous or related – or indeed sufficient explanation of his condition? Symptoms of syncopal attacks appeared long before the myocardial ischaemia and coronary thrombosis which occurred in 1964, as well as before the other symptoms.

The reports submitted by other doctors, and in particular those of Mr Griffiths's own physician, were discounted. 'The members of this tribunal do not agree with the GP's statements and opinions.'

The result of this tribunal was that compensation was reduced from the board's suggested £467 to £1.75 'for lack of vision'. *One pound and seventy five pence.*

Dr Hunter had spoken to Tom Griffiths on the telephone on 30 July 1974 and had said:

> In my view tribunal adjudicators are reasonable and helpful people, who will accept that I have written the absolute truth.

He said that, in view of the evidence of the medical board's findings, he felt sure that the lawyers would be proved wrong and that the decision for full compensation would be upheld by the tribunal. He then asked Tom to tell him the outcome of the tribunal. (Dr Hunter died in December 1978. When he had appeared as an expert witness for Dr Mary Whittaker against ICI she won the case, and was granted several thousand pounds' compensation.)

The Ombudsman's report (on Tom's case) which was completed in November 1978 was long and thorough. However, the importance of the low blood cholinesterase levels recorded at Nancekuke does not appear to have been appreciated and a number of medical facts seem to have been overlooked. The main points which emerged were:

> 1. that a main cause of the failure of Tom Griffiths's case against the Ministry of Defence was the length of time the proceedings continued – 1970 to 1974.

2. that the Ombudsman does not appear to be aware of letters from the Ministry of Defence to Tom Griffiths forbidding him to divulge the facts of his work to anyone, neither does he appreciate the vital importance of the fact that there was a gap of over one whole year in the official records of Tom Griffiths's blood cholinesterase levels.

The fact that Dr Bidstrup pronounced on Tom's case in 1971 without examining him and without mentioning the lowering of his blood cholinesterase level over fifteen months, is disgusting, especially when her evidence alone was responsible for two Secretaries of State for Health refusing to give him compensation.

The Ombudsman quotes from one Ministry of Defence document which mentions a '100 gallon vessel' at Nancekuke and says 'this gives an indication of the scale of operations' and indeed must be considered as a revealing comment upon the need for secrecy which has operated against Tom Griffiths all along.

A journalist, Douglas Carnegie, who has taken great interest in the case and who has helped Tom and Eileen Griffiths in a number of ways, suggested that Eileen write about her experiences of her husband's disability. This document was sent to Dr Kazantzis of the Middlesex Hospital who postponed his report for a further medical board in order to study it.

Dr Kazantzis examined Tom again on behalf of the Department of Health and Social Security on 8 May 1979. He reported that, in his opinion, the majority of Tom's symptoms resulted from his exposure to an organophosphorus compound.

The medical tribunal, which met on 12 June, confirmed this finding, and Tom Griffiths has been offered a permanent pension for life, plus a back payment of £2000 for disability due to nerve gas poisoning.

The struggle has lasted ten years, and could not have succeeded without the support of David Mudd. As it is, Tom had twenty-one years of sickness without treatment or compensation.

How many other cases will now come to light? We know that two people claim permanent disability, and that five employees of

Nancekuke have died, all during the late 1950s and early 60s. That is what we *know* . . .

Reports appeared in the summer of 1969 of large numbers of seal pups dying off the Cornish coast around St Agnes Head, not far from Nancekuke.

A man named Ken Jones ran a seal sanctuary at St Agnes and had cared for sick and injured seals for many years. He was an expert on the colony of grey seals that lives along that coast and on the rocks and islands offshore. Ken Jones was concerned both by the extraordinary numbers of dead and dying seals, and the symptoms they were showing. He described convulsions, burns on the body and burnt out eyes. In his estimation 30 per cent of all seal pups were affected. When I saw reports that these seals were dying of starvation I rang the Marine Biological Association in Plymouth, and was told that fish were very plentiful that summer, and that starvation was extremely unlikely. Neither does starvation cause the symptoms described by Mr Jones.

Eventually the Natural Environment Research Council sent down an expert on seals, a Nigel Bonner, who was quoted in *The Guardian* of 20 December as saying that he believed the cause was starvation.

Many seal experts took up the battle, and one letter to *The Guardian* of December 1969 would seem to express the general opinion cogently:

Sir,
The 30 per cent starvation mortality among pups Mr Nigel Bonner (10 December) so confidently ascribes to the grey seal colony is difficult to credit even as an estimate.
Deaths of young pups from starvation is characteristic of densely crowded colonies, such as that on the Farne Islands studied by Dr J.C. Coulson of Durham University. He found that pre-weaning pup mortality (including causes other than starvation) ranged from nine per cent to 20 per cent as the density of the pups on the shore increased.
The conditions of crowding on the Farne Islands certainly do not occur along the Cornish coast and a level of deaths due to starvation such as has been reported this year is most definitely not 'normal' for Cornwall. For a highly placed official of the Natural

Environment Council (the organisation responsible for advising the government on conservation matters) to make statements such as those of Mr Bonner is a most disturbing development.

Yours sincerely
Susan C. Wilson, Linacre College, Oxford

Other reports, possibly connected with Nancekuke, came to light, concerning the 'sonic barrier' which Cornish skin divers claimed existed over a long period off the coast around Nancekuke. One such professional diver was Geoffrey Upton who was quoted by a local newspaper as saying that he had experienced these undersea noises on many occasions while diving off the coast near Portreath and had assumed it was connected with the experimental station. The phenomenon was well-known to skin divers, and caused pain in their ears.

Dr David Kerr MP (Labour, Wandsworth) tabled questions on 9 May 1968 'following reports that swimmers off the village of Portreath had suffered ear damage by the use of a sonar signal'.

He was answered by John Morris, Ministry of Defence (Equipment) who said:

> the effects of underwater transmissions on divers had been examined in detail by a sub-committee of the Medical Research Council (Carshalton) who reported 'The transmissions referred to, which are being carried out by the Navy Department for oceanographic research purposes and have no connection with the CDE at Nancekuke, could cause no more than minor and temporary discomfort even to skin divers with no ear protection in the immediate vicinity.' (sic) (*The Guardian*, 9 May 1968)

Dr David Kerr also asked if MPs could be given facilities to visit the experimental station at Nancekuke, and was told that MPs could not be given such facilities 'because a significant part of the role of the station is secret'. (John Morris, 9 May 1968.)

The Ministry of Defence eventually reconsidered their decisin, and in October 1970 opened the gates of Nancekuke to the press. (See Chapter 8.)

However, one serious point must be considered. It was raised by Anthony Wedgwood Benn, the then Minister of Technology in

1970. I was in communication with Anthony Benn by letter on the subject of CBW, and I had asked him to make inquiries of the Ministry of Defence as to why Nancekuke had been in large scale production of nerve agents for more than ten years. (I had derived this information from several sources, but due to the Official Secrets Act they must remain undisclosed.) The newspapers reported the following answer:

> Mr Healey said of [my] claim: 'This seems to imply that we have manufactured it in quantities necessary for a capability to wage chemical warfare. We have no capability for chemical warfare, no plans to acquire one, and no stockpiles. The only facilities we now maintain [1970] are on the small scale required to produce quantities of nerve agents which may be required for defensive research.'

What of the '100 gallon container' at Nancekuke, quoted in the Ombudsman's report? Denis Healey has not answered the question. If we have no capability for chemical warfare or plans to acquire one then what does the claim of 'doing it all for our defence' mean?

Why *was* Nancekuke in full scale production for more than ten years? If we have 'no stockpiles', where did it all go?

The hand-out I was given on press open day at Nancekuke stated 'the [nerve gas] plant was designed on "continuous flow" [as opposed to "batch"] principles. When on full stream it had a potential of 13 pounds per hour.' For a *decade*.

The end of the Nancekuke saga is at least hopeful. Tom Griffiths's courage in daring to stand up and tell the truth resulted in many facts about Nancekuke coming to light, and in 1979 an international group of 22 eminent scientists and diplomats visited the plant. The purpose of their visit was 'aimed at demonstrating that verification of the closure and dismantling of former nerve gas plants is possible and acceptable'.

This official press release from the Foreign Office continued:

> It is possible to verify that a chemical plant producing phosphorus compounds for civil use is not, at the same time, producing materials for nerve gases.

To this end the group of scientists also visited a phosphorus producing chemical plant – Albright and Wilson – in Birmingham.

The Ministry of Defence, which had announced plans for the closure of Nancekuke in 1976, has said that the plant will be finally dismantled and evacuated by 1980; it is to become a NATO radar station in the late 1980s.

4

CS Gas

Harassing agents, which include tear gases, were widely used in the first world war and, by the second world war, had been produced and stockpiled in large amounts by the Germans, British, Japanese and Americans, among others. These agents were mainly CN, a lachrymator (tear producing) and DM, or adamsite, a sternutator (irritant acting upon the nasal passages). In 1928 two scientists in the United States, Corson and Stoughton, had synthesised a lachrymator which later bore their initials (CS), but no-one seems to have been very interested in this substance until the early 1950s, when the disadvantages of CN and DM led to a search for a more effective harassing agent. CN (o-chloroacetophenone) is a solid, generally disseminated as a particulate aerosol. The field concentration needed to produce its harassing effects is above ten milligrams per cubic metre, which is high, and proved to be one of its disadvantages; it is relatively unstable chemically and has a low melting point (52°C) which makes it impractical in tropical climates.

DM (adamsite, 10-chloro-5, 10-dihydrophenarsazine) is an arsenical sternutator, which was developed during the first world war. Its high toxicity made it unacceptable for civilian purposes.

CS (orthochlorobenzylidene malononitrile) was developed as a replacement for CN for police use.

> ... it was the culmination of a search for a compound having a more potent irritant action than CN, but less likely to cause complete incapacity than ... arsenical sternutators. After successfully being tried out by police forces, it has been used as a military harassing agent. (*Health Aspects of Chemical and Biological Weapons*, World Health Organisation, 1970.)

Three forms of CS have been developed. The first form is

CS1, a micronised powder formulation containing five per cent of silica gel, for dissemination by explosive burst or dusting apparatus; the second is CS2, to be used in the same way as CS1, and consisting of the latter microencapsulated with silicone to improve its flow properties and weather resistance. CS1 is effective for about a fortnight, while CS2 is considerably more persistent. (US Department of the Army, 1969.)

The third form, the commercial (civil) product is a white crystalline solid which melts at 94-95°C, and is almost insoluble in water. It is used in grenades or cartridges in conjunction with a pyrotechnic mixture which expels the CS in the form of a vapour that immediately condenses to form minute droplets or particles. Obviously it possesses a greatly diminished persistence compared with the military forms CS1 or CS2.

According to the British patent (no.967660) one part per million of CS in the atmosphere will 'incapacitate or strongly subdue unprotected people'. Its effects are:

> In addition to causing pain in the eyes, tears and spasms of the eyelids, CS also produces a sharp burning pain in the nose, throat and chest, which becomes worse and causes a choking sensation as exposure continues. Profuse salivation and running of the nose occur at the same time. Breathing... is rendered extremely painful ... in high concentrations the violent coughing which is set up may induce vomiting. Stinging occurs on the shaved areas, and any exposed abrasions, and there may also be irritation round the neck and other sweaty parts...

That is the British sales talk for CS.

There has been some controversy over the classification of CS; lately the British government has maintained that it is a 'smoke', though the reasons for this would appear to be political rather than technical.

After the appalling misuse of CS by the Royal Ulster Constabulary in the Bogside area of Londonderry, Northern Ireland, in August 1969 it was essential for the British government to restate its attitude to CS in relation to the Geneva protocol, which Britain had signed and ratified. Note must be taken of the pronouncement in 1968 in the House of Commons by Mr Buchan (Under-Secretary of State for Scotland) that the use of CS was 'only to deal with armed criminals or violently insane persons in buildings from which they cannot be dislodged without danger of loss of life, or as a means of self-defence in a desperate situation, and that in no circumstances should it be used to assist in the control of disturbance.'

The term 'smoke' is a misnomer. Early in 1969 the booklet printed for an open day at Porton had a section headed 'Tear Gases', which included CS and described it unequivocally as an 'incapacitating agent . . . several times safer to use than CN'. An American army manual (Training Circular TC 3-16) from the Headquarters of the Department of the Army, April 1969, differentiates between the riot control agents (mostly referring to CS, and described in chapter 2 of the manual) and smoke equipment, described in chapter 4, as a means of obscuring or screening troop activities.

The manual states: 'Smoke is a valuable complement to other weapons and munitions systems . . . it has been used extensively for signalling and screening. In conjunction with the use of the M106 riot control agent disperser (Mighty Mite) and riot control agents there is often a desire to use smoke grenades.'

This would appear to make a clear and precise definition of the function of the two substances. However, in Geneva at the disarmament conference (involving 25 nations) of 19 February 1970, Lord Chalfont told delegates: 'modern CS smoke is not significantly harmful to man in other than exceptional circumstances, and Britain therefore regards it as outside the scope of the 1925 Geneva protocol'.

Again, in the House of Lords on 26 February 1970, Lord Chalfont maintained his stance in the face of questions from Lord Brockway and Lady Wootton. His position appeared to be unenviable, and *The Guardian* of 21 February 1970 reported:

> Lord Chalfont may be considering resignation from his position as Minister for Disarmament, some informed observers believe. The first overt sign that something was wrong behind the scenes in Whitehall was the absence from work of the departmental official in charge of the team which advises Lord Chalfont. He is Mr Ronald Hope-Jones, who is now described as being 'temporarily on leave'.

In fact Ronald Hope-Jones was later moved to another post at his own request.

The Guardian ended its report by saying:

> In Whitehall it is general knowledge that Mr Hope-Jones became convinced there is a strong case for seeking to outlaw CS gas internationally. Lord Chalfont appears to have been convinced of this case as well. When he discussed the problem with Mr Stewart, the Foreign Secretary, Lord Chalfont apparently got clearance to take the idea of a British initiative on war gases – a plan for a total embargo – into Cabinet. But there he found himself in conflict with the Home Secretary, Mr Callaghan, who had sanctioned the use of CS gas in the Northern Ireland disturbances and wanted to retain the widest latitude in its use for crowd control in the future. Mr Healey, the Defence Secretary, appears to have shared this view.

When Lord Brockway questioned Lord Chalfont in the House of Lords he first stated the British government's position:

> For forty years the government has stood for the inclusion of these gases within the terms of the Geneva protocol. Did we not in 1931 secure general agreement at Geneva that lachrymatory gases should be included? What is the reason for this change of attitude?

Lord Chalfont admitted the inclusion of tear gases in 1931, but then made a totally inaccurate statement by way of an excuse:

> Since then the agent CS has been developed. The government decided that this agent was not significantly harmful except in exceptional circumstances, and it was to exclude harmful agents that the Geneva protocol was formulated.

Lady Summerskill then referred to the use of CS in Northern Ireland, and said: 'We sent scientists over there to examine the effects on people who were subjected to it. Those scientists were not unanimous that the gas was harmless.'

I met Lord Chalfont immediately after this debate and, having read in many reputable papers that he was contemplating resigning from his post as Minister for Disarmament and that Ronald Hope-Jones, head of the Department of Disarmament at the Foreign Office was to resign over government policy on CS, I asked Lord Chalfont why he had decided to defend the exclusion of CS from the Geneva protocol. He looked extremely uncomfortable, turned, and waving a hand at Lord Brockway, said, 'Here is your man for morality'.

The press was contemptuous of the government's position, and there were articles headed 'CS and all that smoky gas' and 'Blowing in the wind'. Many scientific and medical publications carried specialist articles on the dangers of mass medication, and of CS in particular.

The lack of information on the toxicity of CS, and the fact that the laboratory tests at Porton and Edgewood Arsenal in Maryland (USA) were carried out only on animals *and* conflicted sharply with each other, made its sale and use particularly questionable.

Both CN and CS were used by the police in the Paris riots of 1968 and Professor Francis Kahn of La Boisière hospital voiced his concern that the toxicity of CS was unknown in France. He claimed that he was treating patients with damage to the cornea, and considered that it was an extremely toxic product. Request for the publication of the findings at Porton on the toxicity of CS were ignored until the Himsworth Committee was set up at Denis Healey's request after the Bogside bombardment, when the editor of the *Lancet* also called for a medical investigation.

Morally and legally the whole question of employing a chemical substance which has not been tested for long-term effects is extremely fraught. The practice of manufacturing, packaging and selling such a substance to other countries for unspecified use is even more morally dubious.

Many people were concerned about CS before the summer of 1969, though the argument put forward that the use of CS in open streets to separate violent factions of rioters, allowing them to disperse and leave the area containing gas – would appear to be rational. Unfortunately its use by the Royal Ulster Constabulary (RUC) in the Bogside riots in August 1969 appears to have been totally irresponsible. The British army handed over undisclosed amounts of CS in grenades, canisters and cartridges to the RUC, apparently with no warnings or instructions as to how to use (or misuse) them.

This resulted in the continuous, 48-hour CS bombardment of a low-lying, densely populated area of a city. The ordinary residents of the Bogside were trapped in their homes. Journalists who spoke to me afterwards were appalled; children were violently sick and had persistent diarrhoea for days, and many old people became extremely ill. The hospitals were full. A doctor to whom I spoke two days after the gas attack had tried repeatedly to obtain medical information from the RUC and the British army, but all he was told was 'when you remove people to fresh air they quickly recover'. At least I was able to tell him what CS gas was, and to pass on advice from a sympathetic and knowledgeable pharmacologist in London.

It was claimed by British observers that at least 1000 rounds of ammunition were used to disperse gas in those two days; one newspaperman, Stephen Markeson said that he saw RUC men using gas rifles long after the crowds had dispersed. He said: 'Constables seemed to be drawing supplies at will from crates stacked in the back of armoured cars. There seemed to be dozens of men armed with gas rifles and I didn't once see an RUC officer controlling the issue of grenades. There was no wind, and the gas hung about in pockets.' He was himself still coughing and sick two weeks after exposure to CS.

The Times of 22 August 1969 reported:

> MPs are frustrated about the difficulties involved in asking Ministers questions about Northern Ireland when the Commons reassembles in October. Any question to Mr Callaghan would be ruled out of order as he is not directly responsible for internal affairs in Northern Ireland. The only way an MP can raise the subject is to question the Prime Minister about the general situation, or to ask the Secretary of State for Defence about troop movements in Northern Ireland.

This whole state of affairs was appalling. MPs could not even raise questions until October because the House was in recess, the Home Office was not in charge of the use of CS gas and the Ministry of Defence was not in command of the RUC. The only democratic way to ensure that the public knew what was happening, and to make those in authority understand how outraged doctors, scientists and the public were, was to persuade the press and television to give as much publicity to the subject as possible. In fact no persuasion was necessary.

In response to the public outcry for facts about the dangers of CS, and for an enquiry about its use and effects specifically in the Bogside, the Home Office asked Sir Harold Himsworth to form an enquiry team to look at the medical aspects of the CS attack. (An enquiry was also instituted into the conduct of the RUC at the time of the Bogside riots, and this resulted in 16 members of the RUC facing charges and a court of inquiry, the outcome of which was never disclosed.)

The Himsworth Committee consisted of Sir Harold Himsworth, former president of the Medical Research Council, Professor Robert Thompson of Middlesex Hospital Medical School (who appeared on the enquiry team looking at Nancekuke and on the Porton advisory panel) and Professor Anthony Dornhorst of St George's Hospital Medical School.

The Guardian of 4 September 1969 reported that these men

> had just completed a day and a half investigation into the effects of the gas on the people of Bogside . . . Sir Harold said: 'We have met nobody who was so incapacitated that he could not pull himself away. There is no evidence that CS gas has produced an illness directly attributable to it among healthy people.'

This statement produced angry letters to the press and some 'sick' cartoons in various publications. *The Guardian* ended its article: 'The enquiry team will fly from Belfast today to Porton Down CDEE to complete their investigations.'

Sir Harold cannot have been quite as sanguine as this report suggests. He asked that there should be a further, thorough enquiry with an enlarged team, and

> that the effects of any chemical agent that might be used for the control of civil disturbances, should be studied from a point of view more akin to that from which we regard the effects of a new drug than to that from which we might regard as a weapon.
> (Command Paper 4173, HMSO, 1969.)

In the second part of this report (Enquiry into toxicological aspects of CS gas and its use for civil purposes, Command Paper 4775, HMSO, September 1971), which James Callaghan had agreed in September 1969 should be prepared, the objective was stated clearly in the second paragraph of chapter 1:

> Public opinion requires that the risks to health that may result from exposure to such agents [CS] shall be substantially less when these are intended for civil control rather than for actual military purposes . . . in the circumstances of civil disturbances, exposure to the agent would not necessarily be restricted to healthy young adults, but might also involve inadvertently others such as children, the elderly and those with impaired health.

The committee then made a most important, if lengthy, point:

> Although our terms of reference are to examine the effects of CS from a point of view 'more akin to that from which we regard the effects of a drug', there is, in our view, an important difference in kind between the assessment of a drug and that of a weapon even when this is intended for civil purposes.
>
> Essentially the acceptability or otherwise of a drug turns upon the balance between the risks and benefits to be expected from its use. If the illness is serious, like cancer, then one is justified in accepting even substantial risks of toxic effects from the drugs employed in its treatment. If, on the other hand, the illness is relatively trivial, then there is no such justification. These are both medical considerations, and the responsibility for striking the balance between them is purely a professional matter.
>
> In the case of a chemical intended for use as an anti-riot agent, however, the considerations to be weighed against each other are different in kind. Some are purely medical: the assessment of the risks to health involved in using the agent in question. Others raise questions of social policy, and must be assessed on political as well as medical grounds.
>
> We have, therefore, conceived of our task as that of making a professional assessment of the risks attendant on the use of CS in order that parliament and the public could be in a position to take an informed decision as to whether or not its use should continue to be sanctioned for riot control purposes.

This last point is one which our anti-CBW campaign had been making for some time and one that has still not been recognised. No debate along these lines has taken place. (I will return to the political and social questions later.)

Meanwhile the World Health Organisation had published their consultant's report on *Health Aspects of Chemical and Biological Weapons* (1970) giving data for the toxicity of CS:

Experimental LCt$_{50}$ values have been obtained in a variety of laboratory animals. For CS aerosols made up of particles of 1.5 micron mass median diameter, these range from 8300 milligrams per minute per cubic metre for guinea pigs up to 43,000 milligrams per minute per cubic metre for mice (Punte et al., 1962). The published estimates of lethal doses for man vary from 25,000 milligrams per minute per cubic metre up to 150,000 mg-min./m^3.

In this connection, it may be noted that estimates of lethal doses for man are likely to be more unreliable for the harassing agents than for any other CW agents. They can be made only by extrapolation from results obtained with laboratory animals.

Now Himsworth (1971) notes that 'the symptoms shown by animals are far less severe than those in man'. But, he continues, 'This relative insensitivity to the distressing effects of CS does not imply that they are insusceptible to its toxic action. This is shown by the finding that animals exposed to high doses have severe internal injuries attributable to this.'

Another finding is surprising. 'A higher concentration for a short time is less toxic than a lower concentration for a long time.' When considering the effects of repeated exposures:

> Once this process of injury has been set in train continuation of exposure produces damage more readily so that it progressively outstrips the processes of recovery . . . exposures to sub-lethal concentrations on several consecutive days can eventually produce a fatal effect.

These last statements in relation to the process of testing CS on human volunteers are extremely disturbing. Both at Porton in England and Edgewood Arsenal (USA) many young service volunteers have been used in experiments with CS (as well as a variety of other CW agents). They were aged between 18 and 30 and received payment of £1 per minute of exposure. Himsworth reports: 'It was found that men could become habituated to the effects of low concentrations of CS.' Habituation implies repeated exposures.

> Tests carried out at Edgewood Arsenal in the late 1960s showed a marked difference in racial sensitivity to CS, just as was shown with mustard gas half a century before. When exposed to high levels of

> CS (14-18 mg-min/litre) the forearms of negro volunteers merely developed local reddening of the skin a few hours after exposure, white-skinned volunteers when treated similarly also developed reddening which led to serious blistering within a few days; extensive scarring was present six weeks after the initial exposure. (Dr Robert Jones, biochemist, Royal College of Surgeons.)

Sir Harold Himsworth, describing the procedure for testing at Porton says:

> Every individual was given a full medical examination . . . before and after exposure, and many were examined 24 hours later . . . on exposure all the subjects found the effects distinctly unpleasant. One subject refused to continue after eight minutes, another left precipitately at 55 minutes in order to vomit.

These volunteers were exposed to very low concentrations, but for dangerously long periods. How many times did they suffer exposure?

This information does not equate with the statement made by Eric Haddon (then Director of CDEE, Porton) in the BBC documentary 'A Plague on Your Children'. He said: 'It [CS] has been tested against aged people, asthmatic people, young people, etc.'

The WHO report has the last word. 'No studies have yet been published on the long-term effects in man of exposure to CS, despite the increasing use of this agent by police and military forces throughout the world.' Himsworth supports the statement, if in a slightly less positive form.

The Stockholm International Peace Research Institute (SIPRI) monograph 'Delayed toxic effects of chemical warfare agents', 1975, says in chapter 4:

> It ought to be pointed out that the toxicological hazards of CS have often been underestimated. Attention should also be paid to the allergenic properties of CS and other riot control agents because of their obvious significance particularly for workers and military personnel employed in production works and stores . . . The question of delayed lesions caused by lachrymators need to be examined. The psychogenic constituent of lachrymator effects should also be given due consideration. The fact remains that lachrymators may cause permanent eye lesions, even blindness. It would be irresponsible to belittle their effects.

Dr Robert Jones (Royal College of Surgeons) is deeply concerned at the possibility of residual lung damage, and in common with others wants to know more of the possibilities of long-term kidney and liver damage. Dr Jones states:

> The self-combustible mixtures used by the authorities also contain kaolin, ostensibly as an inert absorbent material. Kaolin consists of tiny siliceous particles, a proportion of which is very likely to be released in conjunction with the agent. Such a result would enhance both the irritant and damaging effects of CS. Damage certainly does occur. When animals are exposed to aerosols, the small particles of CS cause not only bleeding of tiny sacs where gas exchange occurs in the lungs, but also local patches of cellular death at sites of impact of the particles. Despite controlled exposures of numerous human volunteers no tests of interference with lung function appear to have been performed. The problem lies in assessing the permanence, if any, of the damage. In cases of sub-lethal exposure to certain war gases . . . the lungs eventually heal, but the scars that remain are in a state of contraction. Sudden increases in blood pressure, not uncommon in almost any individual, lead to further bleeding and still more scarring. A vicious circle is thereby set up, the scarring of the lung tissue becoming progressively worse well after the actual exposure.

I shall return now to the social and political implications of the use of chemical agents to control civilians, using the example provided by the battle of the Bogside. It is difficult to evaluate the factors involved, as there might appear to be an element of support for IRA activities seen in any criticism of the British government or the Ulster constabulary's handling of this situation. Such an accusation would be unjustified. The treatment of the civilian population was ill-considered, irresponsible and over-zealous by any standards, and when considered objectively, also proved to be politically ineffective. From many conversations I have had with Irish people of the most moderate view, it may well have been counter-productive in the long run.

The British Society for Social Responsibility in Science (BSSRS) sent Professor Hilary Rose and Russell Stetler (both social scientists) to Londonderry, with a team which included Professor Francis Kahn of the Sorbonne medical faculty, Dr Norman MacDonald, a chest physician and Professor Jack

Mongar, a pharmacologist. (Professor Kahn had had extensive experience of the effects of CS, as he had cared for patients in May 1968 in the Paris riots.) This team was to assess the medical and social effects of a gas attack upon a community, to discover how doctors in the area had been able to cope with such an emergency, and to examine the clinical and toxicological evidence.

They arrived in the Bogside on 13 September 1969 and had a meeting with about a dozen doctors practising there; evidence came to light of political activists who had been extremely reluctant to ask for medical help, or enter hospital, and several of the injured Catholics had asked to be sent across the border to hospital for fear of the police getting hold of lists of patients. The survey was reported in *New Society* on 25 September 1969 and appeared to be the only social/medical survey carried out.

The ITV 'World in Action' team came up with some startling facts about the countries to whom the British government sells CS gas, including a large amount sold and despatched to Rhodesia. We have the right to know if we are selling riot gas to the white Rhodesians, or to anyone else for that matter, and the duty to insist upon such an answer being given.

According to Andrew Wilson, defence correspondent of *The Observer* (15 February 1970): 'It is not too late for the government to change its mind about CS. The argument which raged in the Cabinet throughout December and January is proof of the strength of feeling among Ministers.'

In case of civil strife, is it inevitable that the rule of arms is paramount?

I wrote to Hugh Scanlon, then leader of the AUEW, pointing out that members of his union worked at Nancekuke on the manufacture of CS (among other things) and surely therefore the union should express some opinion upon the subject. A secretary wrote back saying that Brother Scanlon noted my remarks.

The Cornish trade unionists asked the Trades Union Congress to obtain facts about the manufacture of riot control gas at Nancekuke. No answer was ever given.

One disturbing incident in 1970 in Northern Ireland was the death of a child who was asleep in his cot when a canister of CS was lobbed into his bedroom. The Home Secretary, then Reginald

Maudling, said: 'Terence McGuigan died as a result of a state of glandular imbalance present since birth, and only exacerbated by CS.' The answer was prompt – and unsatisfactory.

An article was published in *The Guardian* (14 May 1970) under the heading 'Army to use CS gas on open range'. It reported that the Ministry of Defence was to 'allow the use of CS gas in troop training exercises on the Otterburn moors, Northumberland. The first firing of the gas could come next week when exercises at the Otterburn training camp resume.' After several descriptive paragraphs it ended somewhat optimistically: 'Colonel Mumford [the camp's commandant] said a code has been drawn up by range officials which all visiting troops will be expected to obey when using CS to avoid the possibility of clouds of gas drifting on to populated areas.'

Later it was firmly established that Harrier jump-jets were to have been used to spray the area with CS gas. A letter was despatched to the Minister of Defence, the many protests gathered strength and somehow the whole idea faded away. No gas was used over Otterburn moors.

There was a near disaster in Surrey later in 1970, when a plot was uncovered by the police to bomb the factory there which packages CS from Nancekuke into canisters, grenades and cartridges for despatch to overseas markets. This was reported in *The Guardian* on 30 October. There were six men involved in possessing weapons and explosives, and police were told of a plan 'to attack and fire' the CS gas plant at Dorking. What public hazard this would have caused is quite beyond the imagination, for not only is there CS at Nancekuke, but stocks of mustard gas, and other unnamed substances, which would constitute a major disaster if released over the Cornish countryside.

As a postscript to this chapter I am including the full text of an article published in *The Guardian* of 8 March 1974, called 'Riot control chemical for Ulster camp'.

> The Ministry of Defence has given secret authority to army guards at Long Kesh detention centre, Northern Ireland, to use a new riot control agent in the event of a major disturbance.
>
> The agent, an irritating liquid known as CR which can be fired from water cannon or from hand-held aerosol dispensers, was

first issued to the army in November, but full data on possible harmful side-effects have not so far been published. In a sense, therefore – although the agent has been fully tested on human volunteers of both sexes in Britain and America – the prisoners at Long Kesh could be regarded, and probably will be in Northern Ireland, as guinea pigs.

According to the only available data the agent – whose chemical name is dibenzoxazepine – is highly irritating to skin, eyes and mucous membranes of the nose and throat.

People exposed to even small concentrations are generally forced to close their eyes tightly because of the intense pain, and lose a large degree of physical coordination. The report also says 'due to the severe irritation and a temporary inability to see clearly, some individuals may be expected to develop hysteria'.

This raises the alarming possibility that the agent will prevent rioters from running away at the onset of the spraying, rendering them liable to exposure to heavy concentrations of CR and possible injury. In this sense CR differs from the riot control smoke, RE, whose prime effect is to force rioters to run from the smoke clouds.

The irritant was discovered by chemists at the then Salford Technical College in 1960, and appeared in technical literature two years later. The Ministry's Chemical Defence Establishment at Porton Down took an interest in the mid-1960s when it became apparent that CR, if used for riot control, might be more discriminating than CS, and have a less 'radicalising' tendency on exposed communities.

'Radicalising' has been a particularly disturbing side effect of the use of CS in Northern Ireland, where entire communities have become affected by a smoke fired simply to disperse a small mob. It is often thought the use of CS in 1969 and 1970 contributed largely to the alienation of much of the Roman Catholic population of Belfast and Londonderry.

Development of CR continued at Porton until the late 1960s when, under defence technology agreements, information was given to the United States. The US army carried out tests to see how troops would be affected by exposure to varying concentrations. In September 1972, the surgeon-general of the US army approved its full riot control use.

The US army has been equipped with CR only recently. Its technical report remains heavily classified. The Americans say they cannot release the data because the substance is British. The British say they cannot release the report because tests were made by the Americans.

British scientists submitted a paper on their findings to the

Ministry in 1971. But the Ministry refused permission to publish.

Nothing appeared until October 1973, when a three page paper, written by two Porton scientists and an army doctor, appeared in the journal *Medicine, Science and the Law*. Almost simultaneously the Ministry said the agent would be given immediately to the army, though it did not specify where it might be used.

Yesterday it was learned from Ministry sources that permission had been given for CR to be used in one place only – Long Kesh. Troops guarding detainees are understood to be about to receive, or to have received, hand-held dispensers containing CR.

In January 1978, the then Foreign Secretary Dr David Owen spoke to the Plymouth Fabian Society, and in answer to a question from an Iranian student he admitted that he had authorised the sale of riot control gas and equipment to the Shah of Iran's troops, giving the same excuse as ever – 'If we didn't sell it to them somebody else would.'

5

Research and Experiments

Since the late 1940s accusations and counter-accusations have been made about experiments with biological weapons. A Japanese writer was described by the *New York Times* (16 July 1955) as having witnessed tests in which 3500 human guinea pigs died as a result of biological warfare experiments at a centre near Harbin in Manchuria, then Japanese territory. This was disguised as a Red Cross unit, and was hurriedly destroyed in 1945 when the Russians joined the war in that area.

The diseases being investigated by the Japanese included plague, cholera, typhoid, paratyphoid and anthrax. Chinese and Soviet prisoners were said to have been used in experiments.

An accusation was made in 1949 that the US had experimentally produced an epidemic among Canadian eskimos by means of a biological weapon.

The Soviet Union accused non-communist countries – the United States in particular – of experimenting with biological weapons in the early 1950s, and the US was accused of testing such weapons in Korea.

In 1952 an international scientific commission was asked to investigate the accusations that the USA had been attacking North Korea with biological weapons. Their findings were far from conclusive as there was much confusion over claims that animal and insect vectors – carriers of disease or infection – had been employed (a most unsatisfactory method for a large scale attack). But they did mention their suspicion that a biological aerosol had been used to start an epidemic of encephalitis.

In the 1950s there was a strong (though small) lobby in the US army chemical corps which was convinced that their weapons were to be taken seriously as 'weapons of the future'. The claims made for them ranged from economic to humane, though of course they needed a lot of money to prove their point with a full research and testing programme. They advertised 'war without death'. Luckily some American journalists exposed the whole campaign for the tasteless propaganda that it was.

A most telling letter by John Barden published in the US *Bulletin of Atomic Scientists* in February 1961 says: 'Last April I dropped in on proceedings of the American Chemical Society, called "Symposium on Non-Military Defence, Chemical and Biological Defence in Perspective".'

First a member of the American Medical Association, Dr Harold Lueth, described the symptoms of nerve gas poisoning, and ended 'death may supervene'. Great emphasis appears to have been placed on the cheapness of such weapons, and the fact that none of them destroy property.

A most unpleasant note was struck by George Rich of the (US) Office of Civil and Defence Mobilisation:

> The OCDM has developed prototype gas masks and baby containers for the civilian population. Impermeable family shelters with hand-cranked air and water filters are under development. These items will be put into production and sold through regular retail channels, to paying customers.

Finally, Paul Weiss of the Rockefeller Institute said, 'We must convince the scientific community that chemical and biological warfare is not a dirty business. It is no worse than other means of killing.'

A report from the Committee on Science and Astronautics to the House of Representatives in the US in July 1959 strongly recommended greater support for the CBW programme, and by 1961 it was receiving 57 million dollars with an additional 46 million for the army, but by 1964 the research and development was costing rather more than 158 million dollars, with the army having 117 million, the navy 11 million and the air force 8.7 million for the procurement of actual weapons.

The finances for Porton here in the UK are rather more difficult to ascertain. One of the early activities of the Microbiological Research Establishment (MRE) – part of Porton – during the second world war was the spraying of the island of Gruinard, off the north west coast of mainland Scotland, with anthrax bacillus. Dr C.E. Gordon Smith (Director of Bacteriological Warfare, Porton) has stated that this experiment was instrumental in persuading experts that a biological attack was a feasible military proposition.

The biological activities at Porton did not gain much attention until 1954 when a field test, about which we know very little, was conducted near the Bahamas, and again in 1962 when two members of the Porton staff were found to be suffering from plague.

Plague is caused by a bacterium (pasteurella pestis) which is transmitted via fleas from about 200 different kinds of rodent, the most famous being the black rat.

The disease occurs in three forms. Pneumonic plague affects primarily the lungs and is caused by the bacteria being inhaled. Bubonic plague produces a red rash, swellings of the lymph glands (called buboes) and at its most agonising stage these buboes burst. Septicaemic plague is caused by the bacteria attacking the bloodstream and producing dark discolourations of the skin – hence the name Black Death. Untreated, all three forms are fatal within 24 hours. In the Middle Ages 80 per cent of those who caught the disease died – and in Europe more than 30 million people caught it. Once the plague had a grip in Europe there were recurrent outbreaks until the sixteenth century, and then in 1664 came another epidemic, the Great Plague.

Fleas are not the only means by which plague is spread. If the lungs of a plague victim become heavily infected, bacteria may be exhaled, become airborne, then may be inhaled by another, producing pneumonic plague in the second victim. In this way plague may be passed directly from person to person. Hence the aerosol principle of spreading biological weapons.

Plague was only one of the diseases which interested scientists at Porton in the 1960s. There were at least 160 diseases considered as possible weapons, including eleven of which were thought to be especially suitable: Venezuelan equine encephalitis, tick-borne encephalitis, typhus, Rocky Mountain spotted fever, Q fever, tularaemia, anthrax, brucellosis, plague, typhoid and melioidosis. This last disease is apparently resistant to most antibiotics.

These diseases are bacterial, and therefore vaccines against them do exist, giving protection to the forces employing the weapons.

One aspect of biological warfare was graphically pointed out by US General Rothschild in the BBC film 'A Plague on Your Children'. He was filmed standing near a window overlooking a large American city, and he waved his hand towards this view and said 'If just 30 per cent of these people were ill the medical facilities would be unable to cope.' Indeed he was right.

In Britain the experiments carried out by the microbiological establishment at Porton were lamentable. The over-enthusiastic scientists with quite sizeable amounts of government money had not only infected a Scottish island with anthrax, rendering it unapproachable for a hundred years, but had also involved patients and doctors at St Thomas's Hospital in a grotesque experiment. This was first reported at length in the *British Medical Journal* (vol.1 pp.258-266, 1966). This paper is called 'Leukaemia and neoplastic processes treated with Langat and Kyasanur Forest disease viruses', and was written by Webb, Wetherly-Mein, Gordon Smith and McMahon.

H.E. Webb was consultant neurologist and senior lecturer at St Thomas's Hospital and Medical School; G. Wetherly-Mein was Professor of Haematology at St Thomas's. C.E. Gordon Smith was director of the Microbiological Research Establishment (MRE) at Porton, and Dolores McMahon was Senior Scientific Officer, MRE, Porton.

This article describes how terminal leukaemia and cancer patients were infected – with their consent – with Langat virus and Kyasanur Forest disease. The authors reported that over a four year period 33 patients were treated in St Thomas's and that 'temporary therapeutic benefit was observed in four patients'. All of them subsequently died.

Two patients contracted encephalitis, which causes inflammation and swelling of the brain, and may result in permanent brain damage or death.

One reason given for infecting these terminal patients with

dangerous diseases was said to be 'to decrease the number of white corpuscles in the blood'. Leukaemia massively increases the number of white corpuscles.

The Sun (22 June 1968) published an article headed 'Porton and 33 hospital patients'. The reporter, Malcolm Stuart, began by asking 'Are germ warfare scientists from Porton experimenting with hospital patients?' He continued:

> The Patients' Association is seeking an answer because a Malayan monkey disease given to leukaemia victims in an attempt to provide some relief has since been classified by American and Swedish experts as a potential germ warfare weapon. Last year [1967] an American expert from the US version of Porton – Fort Detrick, Maryland – listed Kyasanur Forest disease as a potential germ warfare weapon, with a 28 per cent mortality rate.

Why were Gordon Smith and McMahon allowed to treat patients in St Thomas's Hospital, and what were the links, if any, between their research and the American report?

Adding to this unsavoury series of events came an item in *The Guardian* of 10 May 1969, reporting that Richard D. McCarthy (the anti-CBW member of the US House of Representatives) accused the US army of testing a rare and lethal kind of encephalitis, a sleeping sickness called Venezuelan equine encephalitis, for germ warfare purposes. McCarthy was reported as saying: 'The army has apparently been testing Venezuelan equine encephalitis for the first time in the United States.' He claimed that it was being tested in Utah (where 6400 sheep were killed by escaping nerve gas in 1968). He said, 'The sleeping sickness disables the brain and can be fatal.'

The United States' arsenal of biological weapons apparently boasted seven 'viable' forms of encephalitis by 1969. Were patients in St Thomas's Hospital unknowing contributors to the research necessary for the inclusion of Kyasanur Forest disease in the list of 'viable weapons'?

Helen Hodgson, chairperson of the Patients' Association, said:

> We believe that human experiments should be conducted with the greatest caution. The ethical problems are particularly serious

> when biological warfare is involved. We have written to the [then] Minister, Mr Kenneth Robinson, to ask if Porton has been conducting any experiments at other National Health Service hospitals. The Medical Research Council brought out a set of recommended rules in 1964 for testing new research on patients. We would like to know of any experiments involving Porton since then.

Did any MP take up this case? Copies of the article were sent to (the Liberal MP) David Steel, and also to William Hamilton (Labour, Fife). What action, if any, was taken?

On 28 January 1970, *The Guardian* carried the following story headed 'Ministry denies killing old people after experiment'. It was written by John Kerr, and said that the Ministry of Defence had described as 'ludicrous' a suggestion that old people had been used as 'guinea pigs' for experiments, and quietly put to death afterwards. The allegation was made by Monsignor John Barry, the Rector of St Andrew's Roman Catholic College, Drygrange, Melrose, Scotland, in a speech about the problems of the aged, made to the Edinburgh City Business Club.

He claimed:

> I have seen evidence which I think is genuine, although I cannot guarantee this, that there is a certain section of the Ministry of Defence which uses elderly people as guinea pigs for experiments, and quietly puts them to death afterwards. It is carefully hidden by the Official Secrets Act.

Monsignor Barry said he was sure that the evidence that he was shown was an official document. He could not name the source of his information, or say where the alleged experiments were carried out; but he knew, and that it was in the British Isles. He firmly believed the document to be genuine, its contents being 'sufficient to convince me of its authenticity'. The incidents to which it related had apparently occurred within the previous two years, from 1968 to 1970. He said that he had seen the evidence recently and 'hadn't known what action to take'.

On 6 February 1970 *The Guardian* reported that David Steel (Liberal MP) had met Monsignor John Barry, who gave him the documents to which he had referred in January.

David Steel said that there were certain disquieting aspects of the case which needed investigating. The article continued: 'Mr

Steel spoke yesterday to the private office of Mr Healey (Secretary of Defence) and as a result has passed the documents to him with a covering letter raising queries which Mr Steel has offered to discuss further.' Despite repeated follow ups, there the matter rested.

In the House of Commons on 19 February 1970 Harold Wilson said: 'Claims that the government was putting to death old people after experimenting on them were completely without foundation.' Harold Wilson was answering a question by William Hamilton who asked if the Prime Minister had inquired into 'the monstrous accusations' made by Monsignor Barry.

Wilson said:

> Any government department may from time to time undertake scientific research involving human beings as subjects, in accordance with the volunteer principle. It is the responsibility of the Minister in charge of the department to see that there are fully adequate safeguards for the health and wellbeing of those taking part.

He said that the fullest inquiries had been made into this matter.

Harold Wilson's answers to William Hamilton were ambiguous in the extreme and one can only hope that the hospital in south east England was deterred by Monsignor Barry from pursuing the alleged experiments.

Now I must repeat a quote from the BBC documentary 'A Plague on Your Children'. Eric Haddon, ex-Director of Porton CDEE, twice mentioned using human beings for tests of chemical weapons. He said of CS 'We have no evidence whatever that this agent is lethal. It has been tested against aged people [volunteers?], asthmatic people, young people, etc.' Then, talking about incapacitators (psychochemicals) he said: 'to be sure, tests must also be done on men'. The interviewer then asked him, 'Now when you test on men, as you say, who are you in fact testing on?' Haddon replied: 'We test on volunteers from the three services . . . we are not allowed to go near a killing dose.'

This implies, surely, that what is being tested is potentially lethal. Eric Haddon also referred to tests on asthmatic and aged people, who cannot have been volunteers from the services. Who were they and how and where did they come to be used?

Another aspect of biological weaponry research was demonstrated when a story emerged in 1977 about the use of an animal disease to 'destabilise' the Cuban economy. This operation was undertaken without there being a war, so the Geneva Convention did not apply.

The introduction of African swine fever to Cuba in 1971 by CIA-backed operatives caused an outbreak of the disease which resulted in the slaughter of 500,000 pigs. *The Guardian* (10 January 1977) reported that an unidentified US intelligence source was given an unmarked container of the virus at Fort Gulick, an army base in the Panama Canal zone used by the CIA, and that the container was taken by fishing boat to agents in Cuba.

Swine fever appeared in Havana shortly after, and was the only outbreak ever to have occurred in the western hemisphere. The Cubans relied on raising pigs in their backyards as an important part of their domestic economy, and a loss of 500,000 pigs must have been a heavy blow.

The CIA did not deny these allegations.

A documentary made for the 'World in Action' series (ITV), shown in autumn 1975, was concerned with chemical weapons testing on servicemen in the United States. The substances tested were never clearly specified, though from descriptions of the effects some would appear to be psychochemicals with varying degrees of potency.

One officer was so disastrously affected that he leapt from an upstairs window and was killed outright; President Ford heard of this during the post-Watergate era and invited the officer's family to the White House where he publicly apologised to them.

In 'A Plague on Your Children' GIs were shown suffering from the effects of a chemical that was named as BZ, and is now known to be a psychochemical which has been developed specifically as an incapacitating agent for chemical warfare.

> [BZ] is an anti-cholinergic agent closely related chemically and pharmacologically to such benzillates and other glycolates as ditran and aprofen. Its chemical structure is a military secret, but it is believed to be a phenyl glycolate ester of an aminoalcohol, such as 3-quinuclidinol. BZ is a white crystalline solid, whose physical and chemical properties and thermal stability permit effective aerosols to be generated from pyrotechnic compositions. BZ is apparently

intended for use in aerosol form to create a respiratory hazard. Effective doses can also be absorbed through the skin . . . the symptoms of BZ poisoning are increased heart rate, dry skin and mouth, mydriasis and blurred vision, ataxia, disorientation and confusion progressing to stupor . . . Large inhaled concentrations will produce a progressive intoxication in the untreated casualty as follows: (US Department of the Army, 1967)

1-4 hours: tachycardia, dizziness, ataxia, vomiting, dry mouth, blurred vision, confusion and sedation progressing to stupor.

4-12 hours: inability to respond effectively to environmental stimuli or to move about.

12-96 hours: increasing activity, random unpredictable behaviour; gradual return to normal 2-4 days after exposure.

In the case of percutaneous intoxication symptoms may take as long as 36 hours to appear . . . No information is available on estimates of lethal dosages, or on experimental data with laboratory animals.

BZ apparently possesses the physical and chemical properties that are essential for potential use in chemical warfare, and its cost is considerably less than that of LSD. Effective field concentrations for military purposes seem to be feasible, and weapons have been designed to disseminate it. As an incapacitating agent the principal drawbacks of BZ seem to be unpredictability of its effect on troops in the field, and the severe or even fatal injuries that may result from its use in hot, dry weather. There is no information on the risk of directly lethal dosages being set up in the field, but this is unlikely to be negligible. (*Health Aspects of Chemical and Biological Weapons*, World Health Organisation 1970)

An article appeared in *The Guardian* (2 August 1979) headed 'Delirium Drug Dumped in Ocean'. Evidence given to The United Nations Committee on Disarmament in Geneva accused Britain of conducting BZ research on British servicemen and of disposing of unwanted stocks of BZ in the Atlantic, somewhere 'to the west of Ireland' in 1967. A report prepared for the US Army in 1977 concluded that 'BZ can last up to 135 years before reaching a safe level.'

It was stated that several American servicemen who had undergone tests with BZ between 1963 and 1975 were still suffering severe side-effects, weight loss, dizziness and mental disorientation. BZ is described in American Army papers as quinuclydinalbenzillate, an anticholinergic agent.

The SIPRI monograph *Delayed Toxic Effects of Chemical Warfare Agents* published in 1975 states:

> Although intensive research has been conducted for many years now on the mechanism of action of psychochemicals and has resulted in remarkable findings, the latest publications in this field still provide too little information on the metabolic pathways of such compounds . . . It may be said, on the one hand, there is a great dearth of data on substances with military psychochemical potential, and that, on the other, the experience hitherto gained with model chemicals has plainly shown the great dangers of permanent and delayed lesions. If, contrary to the findings of scientific research, the advocates of psychochemical warfare persist in taking the line that this type of warfare is the most humane they are simply misleading public opinion.

The chemicals now under discussion are known by a variety of names; the military designation of them as 'incapacitators' is too generalised, and they are known more precisely as psychochemicals, hallucinogens, psychedelics or psychomimetics. There are many different substances in this category which have been tried, but the ones most widely known are

1. LSD-d-Lysergic acid diethylamide
2. DMT dimethyltryptamine
3. STP 3-5-dimethoxy 4 methyl amphetamine
4. Psilocybin

These are all substances of high potency, that is, they are extremely effective even in minute quantities (microgram range) and are undetectable in use: no taste, colour or smell.

There appear to have been several aspects of research for psychochemicals: their use for brainwashing or interrogation of prisoners; the short-term intoxicating or disabling effect on troops in the field, and the long-term effects on the human organism produced by repeated doses.

In a book, *The Mind Manipulators* by Alan W. Scheflin and Edward M. Opton Jnr. (Paddington Press 1978), which was reviewed in *New Scientist*, 17 August 1978, the authors state that, 'for the past thirty years the CIA and US army have been experimenting with techniques of mind control'. The CIA and US army commissioned research on drugs, psychological techniques of brainwashing, hypnotism and even brain stimulation.

The authors claim that 'Dangerous drugs including massive doses of LSD were administered to many American citizens without their knowledge.' These statements have never been denied by the CIA or the US army. CIA papers confirming these and other activities concerning 'mind-bending' drugs have been thoroughly investigated by a US Senate committee specifically set up for this purpose in the post-Watergate enquiries into the CIA.

One of the most alarming results of this area of chemical warfare research is the effect it had upon many people in the 1960s. LSD, psilocybin, DMT and STP all 'accidently' became available, were adopted by a Harvard professor of psychology, Dr Timothy Leary, and sold to a generation as the great mind-blowing means of escape from materialism, bureaucracy and the horrors of war.

The United States has been interested in psychochemicals since the 1950s, and we have seen that the ideal chemical weapon would be one which was not lethal but would render the enemy harmless, passive and disorientated.

An article by Michael Carter published in *New Scientist* of 26 August 1976 lends weight to the above. It is called 'Flying high for the US army' and is based upon a US army report released in August 1976. This report relates to LSD, mescalin, psilocybin and STP, and admits that frequently drugs were administered without the knowledge or permission of the subjects or their families and that the army tried to conceal its role in the research. At least two people died as a result of the tests.

In a book called *The Man who Turned on the World* by Michael Hollingshead (Blond and Briggs 1973), there is an account of Timothy Leary giving LSD to 300 people. 'A glance at some of our results suggests that the military applications of consciousness expanding drugs may be limited.' (p.42)

On the same page there is a description of the Leary research project giving LSD to 100 'hardened criminals' in a maximum security prison.

After leaving Harvard, Leary found a patron, a millionaire

called Howard Teague, who gave Leary's group, now called the Agora Trust (A Foundation for Mind Research) large amounts of money to set up a 'cosy, well-equipped' garden flat for their research (p.95). 'We had hundreds of requests from people all over America who wanted to take LSD.' Later, on page 97, Hollingshead says:

> With the establishment of the New York centre, plus a form of status stabilisation with Washington (via the US navy who intervened on our behalf with the Federal Drug Agency by placing our work in a rosy, even golden light) . . . this New York phase ended.

Later another millionaire, Billy Hitchcock, gave the group a 64-roomed house with a 2000 acre walled estate near New York, 'at a nominal rent'.

There is claim made in this book that a psychologist from the National Aeronautics and Space Administration (NASA) gave Leary's group substantial amounts of something called a 'space drug' – JB118 – which, it was said, was officially on the secret list. 'Dick [Alpert] and I volunteered to try it, and remarked that it looked like we were becoming guinea pigs for NASA and the CIA.' (p.125)

Michael Hollingshead also mentions JB840, another coded drug from NASA. He describes this as 'a solid slab of hallucinatory experience that offered nothing for the traveller to bring back to the real world'.

Papers were also published by scientists at Porton Down on the subject of psilocybin and mescalin analogues. The report discloses that the US conducted a massive programme of human testing, with frequent disregard for ethical procedures on the part of the army researchers and civilian programmes funded by the army.

The confusion apparent as to the goals set for this research is clear. The reasons put forward are: to find shorter-acting hallucinogens than LSD, to lower resistance to interrogation, to find suitable antidotes, to provide a combat tool and to provide an alternative to nuclear war.

A statement in the *New York Times* by Dr Van M. Sim, the

civilian director of the US army's programme at Edgewood Arsenal, Maryland, said that experiments with LSD were dropped in 1967 'because the army really wanted a drug that would stun an enemy, but leave it able to carry out orders'.

The only known hallucinogen known to be stockpiled in the United States is BZ.

In 1975 the US army was testing atropine and scopalamine on 55 military personnel at Edgewood Arsenal; it was denied that either drug could cause hallucinations. But the ability of both drugs to cause delirious states has been well known for many years.

In 1973 the US army at Edgewood published a paper showing that the behavioural effects of atropine, scopalamine and ditran (an anti-cholinergic hallucinogen) are indistinguishable from each other. 158 army men were the subjects of the tests.

When Britain's chemical research establishment at Porton held an open day in 1969, a film was shown of British 'volunteers' being used for experiments with psychochemicals.

No tests were done after 1967 (what a strange coincidence – that is when the United States gave up their tests with LSD). The Ministry of Defence said 'the results were so inconclusive'.

When a Ministry spokesperson was questioned about hallucinogenic weapons being stockpiled in Britain he answered that he could not say either way categorically *(The Guardian,* 19 July 1975). But a footnote to this story came from Pendennis in *The Observer* of 20 August 1978:

> The Chinese may be contemplating turning the Russians on with LSD. In a new book Detective Inspector Richard Lee – since retired – reveals that during his enquiries he discovered that a British chemical company supplied China with 400 million dosage units of LSD – enough to paralyse her neighbour for up to 16 hours.

No comment or denial came from any quarter in reply to this charge.

If such weapons are described as 'for use in civilian riots' are they in fact a political weapon for use by the regime in power in situations of political unrest or protest?

The extent of CBW research in American universities, hospitals and colleges has never been established, though one ten-year research programme carried out at the University of Pennsylvania was worth $845,000. Eventually several members of the university faculty threatened to wear gas masks at all university ceremonies unless the contracts were dropped. It was suggested in 1967-68 that more than 50 American universities and colleges had received contracts for research and, of course, industry was even more involved.

The Americans also conducted CBW tests in Panama and Greenland, at Fort Greely in Alaska and Fort Huachua in Arizona. These claims were made by Seymour Hersh in his book *Chemical and Biological Warfare* published in America in 1968. He also claimed that the United States had 22 contracts for CBW research with Japanese universities and medical colleges. 'In the United States CBW is apparently both big business and higher learning.' *(All Fall Down*, Robin Clarke, 1969)

The following story was reported in *The Guardian* of 23 December 1976 by two Washington correspondents:

> At least eight American cities and military installations were subjected to simulated biological warfare attacks by US army scientists between 1950 and 1966. The military continued to use a bacterium that was implicated in an outbreak of infection that killed one man in San Francisco within weeks of the initial tests.

The bacterium, serratia marcescens, was used in tests conducted by the US army in Key West, Panama City, Florida, in San Francisco and finally in New York City, by dispersal in the subway system. The army installations affected were at Point Mugu and Port Hueneme, Fort McClellan, Alabama and a navy facility in Pennsylvania. They also admitted testing bacteria in the Pentagon, but were reluctant to give any details.

Another substance tested in Pennsylvania was a fungus, aspergillus fumigatus which, the army admitted, could be fatal to humans.

The US army said that such tests were abandoned after the executive ban on offensive biological warfare in 1969, but said: 'The biological substances involved in the tests were used as stimulants for training and field evaluation to determine vulnerability to enemy biological attack and adequacy of defence measures.'

One wonders what measures for civilian defence have resulted from such tests upon civilians.

These facts emerged at the hearing of a Senate Select Committee in 1975. One US Defence Department employee, Charles Senseney, described how he dropped a light bulb containing a 'simulant agent' from a moving subway train, 'and the spread of the agent through the subway was monitored'.

Another distasteful aspect of US biological weaponry research was revealed in the *Sunday Times* (13 March 1977) when it was disclosed that the kidneys from aborted foetuses from South Korea were imported 'live' into the US army biological weaponry research centre at Fort Detrick, Maryland.

Professor Lee Myung Bok of the Medical Department at Seoul University said he was paid 15 dollars a pair for the kidneys. Foetal material was imported for such research from 12 countries and was used at the army's Walter Reed hospital and at Fort Detrick.

However we cannot be complacent about Britain's position. One scientist, involved in a protest to Harold Wilson, was quoted by *The Times* as saying (28 June 1968), 'When we take part in exercises with Americans and Canadians in Canada I do not know what happens, and I should think it quite justified to be suspicious about it.'

Some light was shed on these suspicions in a brochure for the Canadian Defence Research Establishment (DRES) of the Defence Research Board at Ralston, Alberta. This establishment is located 28 miles west of Medicine Hat, and includes a test area of 1000 square miles 'complete with access roads, communication systems and distributed power supplies'. The purpose of DRES is to conduct basic and applied research on problems of defence against biological, chemical and nuclear warfare.

Then comes a description of the lavish and comprehensive social and domestic arrangements for the staff of Suffield.

The research wing, in which there are seven sections is then described: 'these laboratories are equipped with research facilities of the highest quality . . . requirements for special equipment can usually be met'.

After descriptions of the Aerophysics and Shock Tube

Section, and the Geophysics and Structures section, the brochure continues:

> The programme of the Physiology section relates to the study of the potential threat of possible agents of chemical warfare. The programme includes studies in biochemical, toxicological and medical fields of research; pharmacological investigations in experimental animals and in human volunteers are emphasised.

Then comes a list of highly sophisticated electronic equipment available, and: 'The programmes are supported by some of the finest animal colonies in Canada.' Elsewhere the brochure states: 'A field trials and analysis group develops sampling and chemical analysis methods, and carries out studies of the behaviour of chemicals dispersed in the field, with relation to defence against chemical warfare.'

The Plans and Reporting section plans the field trials and

> the correlation of findings from the DRES programmes with those from other defence organisations also plays an important role. These activities provide opportunities for operations research and associations with military personnel. [Notably British regiments.]
>
> Close liaison with the Defence Scientific Information Services at Defence Research Board Headquarters and interlibrary loan arrangements with Canadian and foreign government research agencies and establishments make broad literature surveys possible.
>
> The Logistics wing is responsible for the general support and operation of the station, and the organisation and execution of the field trials programme. There are opportunities for those with engineering training who favour outdoor activity, or who are interested in testing and development of weapons.

One thousand square miles for 'engineering activities . . . all directed towards the execution of complex field trials either at DRES or "on safari" '.

The budget for all this was four million dollars a year in July 1967, though this has subsequently been halved.

I wrote to ask the Canadian Prime Minister if British troops had been engaged in field trials at Suffield in June 1968. I received an interim acknowledgement, but no further reply.

There was a report that the UK Black Watch regiment had been involved in training exercises in CBW at Suffield in 1970;

certainly there has never been any attempt to hide the fact that British troops take part in mock nerve gas battles in West Germany. Also twelve senior British officers used to attend courses at the Dugway CBW proving ground in Utah every year.

When the British government refused to disclose the names of foreign powers with research programmes in Britain (May 1968), the US Senate Foreign Relations Committee was more forthcoming. They listed US army research contracts with British universities for 1967 which included ten in chemical and five in biological research.

Tam Dalyell pressed the British government to reveal the number of British CBW research contracts within our own country. Eventually the appropriate select committee was told that in 1968 the CDEE at Porton had 27 contracts with universities and colleges including: King's College, London; Middlesex Hospital Medical School; St Mary's Hospital Medical School; The Institute of Neurology, London; Queen's University, Belfast; the universities of Liverpool, Edinburgh, Southampton, Sheffield, Wales, Manchester, Bristol, Exeter, Kent and St. Andrew's; and with colleges of technology at Cardiff and Portsmouth. The Microbiological department of Porton had contracts with Birkbeck College and the universities of Oxford, Birmingham and Wales, and with the Oxford College of Technology.

(It may be of interest to note that Dr B. Jacques of the Portsmouth College of Technology was studying the synthesis of 4-hydro 1,2,3,4-tetrahydroisoquinolines, which are very similar to other hallucinogens.

Professor J.B. Cavanagh of the Institute of Neurology was said to be studying a group of chemical compounds used in pesticides and insecticides which can cause paralysis. Surely he might have been of assistance in the previously cited cases of alleged nerve gas damage?)

The question of secrecy was answered in the House of Commons by Roy Mason (then a Junior Minister of Defence) on 26 February 1968:

> When arranging a research contract the Ministry of Defence agrees with the university who is to supervise the work . . . The results of research for defence are, in accordance with general scientific

practice, published freely, providing there are no overriding considerations of national interest, including security. Universities undertake to consult the Ministry of Defence before publication. Over the past two years no university has declined to undertake a research contract offered to it.

The then Director of CDEE, Porton, Neville Gadsby, said, in his usual practical vein: 'We do not put the university into a position they do not want themselves . . . the fact is, the money is welcome.'

However the climate of opinion appears to have changed considerably, and if our campaign has helped this one aspect of CBW research I should be delighted. To quote from a letter to *The Guardian* (28 May 1976) from a student protesting about degrees in policy studies at the University of Kent:

> Is your memory so short? Have you already forgotten that during the sixties it was revealed that chemical and biological warfare techniques were being perfected in university laboratories, and that, in the United States, government agencies were financing social science research designed to aid the 'pacification' process in Vietnam?

I hope that his use of the past tense is wholly justified.

In a pamphlet 'The new technology of repression – Lessons from Ireland' produced by the British Society for Social Responsibility in Science (paper 2, 1974), the authors quote the chairperson of the Royal United Services Institute for Defence Studies speaking at a seminar on 'The Role of the Armed Forces in Peacekeeping in the 1970s' held in April 1973, as saying:

> What happens in Londonderry is very relevant to what can happen in London, and if we lose in Belfast we may have to fight in Brixton or Birmingham. Just as Spain in the '30s was a rehearsal for a wider European conflict, so perhaps what is happening in Northern Ireland is a rehearsal for guerilla war more widely in Europe, and particularly in Great Britain.

6

Hazards

The dangers of storage and transportation of chemical agents were coming to light in 1968. The admission by the Ministry of Defence that CS gas was transported by road to the firm of Schermuly in Dorking, and that 'certain agents' which were tested 'on small patches of ground and protective garments' at Nancekuke and then sent to Porton 'in laboratory quantities' gave west country people cause for concern.

The *Plymouth Independent* (2 June 1968) noticed the strange silence of the (then) MP for Camborne, Dr John Dunwoody:

> From the good doctor has come not one single peep about Nancekuke . . . why the silence? a good watch dog should bark. Must we rely on housewives and newspapermen to prod our local watchdog?

The MPs Dr David Kerr, John Pardoe, David Mudd and Alistair MacDonald all asked questions in the House of Commons and eventually, on 23 September 1969, a working party was set up to look into the transport of nerve agents from Nancekuke to Porton, and the disposal of effluent from nerve agent production.

The working party consisted of ten men, of whom three were from the Ministry of Defence: G.N. Gadsby, Director of the Chemical Defence Experimental Establishment, Porton: G.D. Heath, Director of Biological and Chemical Defence: and P. Sansom. Three were on the panel of scientific advisers to Porton: Professor R.H.S. Thompson, Middlesex Hospital Medical School: Professor N.B. Chapman, Hull University, and Dr H.K. Black, who is also the chief Inspector of Explosives for the Home Office. The four remaining members of the working party were: Professor P.J. Garner, Birmingham University: Dr H.W. Ashton, BP

Chemicals; Dr J.M. Barnes, Medical Research Council, Carshalton, and Dr J.A. Storrow of Fisons Ltd.

Their report stated:

> The working party was set up on 25 November 1969 to advise on the potential hazards arising from
> a) the transport of nerve agents by road from Nancekuke to Porton
> b) the disposal of effluent from a nerve gas production facility if it were located at Porton instead of Nancekuke
> We were subsequently invited to advise on the safety of the effluent disposal currently in use at Nancekuke.
>
> We held our first meeting at CDE, Porton Down on 25 November 1969 and our second at CDE Nancekuke on 7 January 1970.

Then the packaging of the nerve agents and the safety precautions taken were described. The report continued:

> We were also given additional information by the directing staff responsible for the safety of the whole operation . . . In the light of our discussions we reached the following conclusions
> a) the conveyance of nerve agents from Nancekuke is carried out in a thoroughly responsible manner and there are no objections on safety grounds to the conveyance under the present CDE regulations of further consignments of nerve agents should they be needed in the future.

Regarding the effluent disposal system at Nancekuke, the report stated:

> We concluded that the effluent disposal system at Nancekuke is entirely satisfactory to treat effluents arising from all foreseeable eventualities, and embraces safeguards not common to normal practice.

However one paragraph left some doubts:

> The toxicities of any chemicals arising from CDE Nancekuke have been determined with respect to small fish, molluscs and prawns indigenous to the area and final effluent is tested against these species before it is disposed of.

The question of dangers arising from the transportation of large amounts of nerve gas was not asked, though in the light of later developments it should have been.

In July 1969 the US *Wall Street Journal* carried reports of nerve gas leaks at the American base of Okinawa at the same time that news had come of hopeful talks at the Geneva disarmament conference on banning chemical and biological weapons in what Mr James Leonard, the United States delegate, described as 'an atmosphere of determination and promise'.

The Guardian, following up the story, reported that VX had leaked from a broken container at Okinawa. 'It is the first word to reach the public that the US is apparently deploying chemical war weapons overseas.' There was no way of suppressing the news that 25 men had been sent to hospital after exposure to nerve gas. The article went on:

> On Thursday night there was an emergency meeting of White House and Defence Department officials, who for a time did little more than sit around and curse the fate that blew the seal off one of the Pentagon's top secrets. The military is in bad odour just now, not only with radicals and student demonstrators but also with Congress as well. The Safeguard ABM is going to have a rough time squeaking through the Senate without people suddenly being reminded of the six thousand sheep that died at a CBW testing range in Utah last year, and of the hullabaloo that arose in the spring when it became known that the army was about to put twenty seven thousand tons of chemical war products on a train and ship them east to be dropped into the ocean off the summer beaches of New Jersey. Now it comes out that lethal gas is deployed on a Japanese island, off which, last summer, a hundred children collapsed from an undisclosed ailment after swimming near the American base.

The Times on 25 July asked 'Could nerve gas be stored in Britain?' Senior officials in Whitehall calmly replied that 'Britain has no agreement which would allow the United States to store nerve gas in this country, and no government is likely to grant permission for it.' This was a less than satisfactory answer. Had the Japanese and West German governments 'granted permission' for VX to be stored? *The Times* nervously concluded: 'Theoretically, therefore, the incident on Okinawa where a leakage of nerve gas injured servicemen, could not take place in Britain.'

Later in that article I am quoted as being concerned at the transportation of nerve gas from Cornwall to Porton: 'The Americans took no fewer precautions than the British, yet an accident had occurred.' On the same day *The Times* leader announced (under the heading 'Nerve gas in Britain') that 'the United States eventually announced a decision to remove poison weapons from Okinawa'. It goes on:

> It is a serious enough disclosure of the suspected but hitherto unconfirmed overseas deployment of chemical weapons by the United States . . . the fact that the Japanese government were clearly ignorant of the existence of this stockpile at Okinawa.

The writer then continues by again asking: 'Do the Americans have facilities here for the storage of nerve gases?' and 'Is there a danger that such leakages could occur in the research programmes which Britain carries out into the same kind of gases?'

Three questions which were *not* asked were:
1. where was the large amount of nerve gas manufactured at Nancekuke during the late 1950s and early 1960s stored?
2. what happened to the 100 children, 25 servicemen and any others who were contaminated during the Okinawa leak? According to our information they could not be cured; were they compensated by the US government for permanent damage?
3. considering the number of protest committees being formed all over West Germany against United States stockpiles of nerve gas in their country *(The Times* had said 'Obviously the Americans deploy such stockpiles elsewhere around the world') how would the Americans react?

No answers were supplied to the first two questions; indeed, has anyone else ever asked them very forcibly? But the answer to the third was appalling. The US government panicked.

In East Anglia on 13 February 1970 an American jet plane leaking 'lethal fumes' had landed at Mildenhall Air Base. The front pages of all the daily papers carried banner headlines. The most dramatic examples were those of the *Daily Express*: 'US base scare – homes cleared', 'Plane drama at Mildenhall. Hundreds evacuated' and 'Mid-air emergency after toxic leak fear'.

By the next day – 14 February – a clearer picture had

emerged, and *The Times* expressed 'Doubts over air base alarm' in more measured terms:

> Some questions remained unanswered when Sergeant Thomas Freeman, who started the alert that led to 2000 people being evacuated on Thursday at Mildenhall, Suffolk, flew back to the United States yesterday.
>
> He was the loadmaster on the Starlifter jet transport which landed at the air base on its way from Germany after it was suspected that toxic fuel was leaking . . . After making an investigation, Mr Eldon Griffiths [Conservative MP for Bury St Edmunds] said: 'It now appears that an indicator was malfunctioning and at no time was there real danger.'

Eldon Griffiths, who had inspected the load, said that there was no nuclear weapon or nerve gas on board. *The Times* continued:

> The suggestion that it was all a false alarm leaves unanswered many questions.
>
> The wearing of gas masks by policemen, and the measures to seal off the doors and windows in the evacuation centres could not be satisfactorily explained even by the original official suggestion that there was a suspected leak in the fuels of the Bullpup missiles which were on the aircraft. A leak of liquid fuel would not have necessitated the scale of precautions unless there were more toxic substances on board.
>
> One can only assume that the possibility of an accident involving nerve gases was thought real enough to justify these precautions.
>
> This does not accord with the agreement Britain has with the United States that such weapons will not be brought anywhere near Britain.

There are many aspects of this occurrence which have never been explained.

As a reporter on *The Guardian* said, the area evacuated around Mildenhall was far greater than would be necessary for any explosion caused by rocket fuel, and any toxic fumes released would have been dangerous inside the confined space of the aircraft, but no further afield.

People in schools half a mile away were told by the police to close all doors and windows and put blankets around the cracks – the reverse of emergency procedures for explosions.

The Guardian said:

> The contradictions argue either that the police were given insufficient information by Mildenhall about the nature of the danger, or . . . there may have been more in the cargo of the C-141 than 'conventional munitions' . . . The US air force constantly ferries equipment and weaponry back to the States for refurbishment. US forces are believed to have deployed chemical weapons in Europe. Cluster bomblet warheads to spread chemical warfare substances have been fitted to the surface-to-air missiles Little John, Honest John and Sergeant.
>
> A version of the Bullpup is being developed to fragment – the standard delivery system for toxic substances. If such weapons are deployed in Europe it seems possible . . . that they too, like other weaponry, are from time to time ferried to the United States for checks.

There are two most significant notes struck by journalists:

1. 'Police toured villages in the line of the easterly wind, telling people to stay indoors and keep the windows closed.' (*Daily Express*, 13 February 1970)
2. 'The jet made a perfect landing and was directed to park on a remote part of the airfield – on hardstanding No. 13. where there were seven tanks holding aircraft fuel? There it was quickly surrounded by men of the emergency services . . . wearing special suits, gas masks and carrying oxygen cylinders on their backs.'

The last quote is from *The Observer* of 15 February 1970: 'The giant Starlifter was not carrying deadly nerve gas, though officers at the base had reason to believe it might be.'

Why did American officers allow an American plane, which they had reason to believe might be leaking nerve gas, to land on British soil? Did the USAF ask permission of the British government to allow such a landing? Has Eldon Griffiths (as the MP for this area) bothered to ask such questions, and have the answers been reassuring for the safety of his constituents?

The Observer continues:

> The elaborate precautions taken, including police warnings to seal doors and windows in the area with blankets, suggest that the plane

was first thought to be one of a fleet removing nerve gas stocks from West Germany to dumps in the US.

They were not welcome there either.

This problem arose, according to Richard Scott in *The Guardian* of 15 December 1969, 'from representations from the Japanese government last summer, after leakage from at least one canister of nerve gas had put a number of civilians in hospital'.

However, President Nixon ordered consignments of VX to be shipped back to the US. Richard Scott continues:

> The next shipment due to leave in the next few days will be unloaded near Seattle, and sent on by train to the Umatilla army depot in eastern Oregon.
>
> The people of Washington and Oregon are deeply disturbed by this development. The Governor and Senator Hatfield have written to President Nixon to protest. Firstly because he has only recently become aware of the fact that lethal gas was already being stored at Umatilla; and secondly that it was to be supplemented by the gas carried by train across his state.
>
> There were nationwide protests early this year when it was discovered that the Army was planning to move surplus stocks across the country by train before dumping them in the Atlantic.
>
> Governor McCall further protested that the US, having agreed not to subject the people of Okinawa to the lethal gas, was now planning to inflict it upon the people of Oregon . . . This was not the end of Mr Nixon's troubles. The West German Chancellor, Herr Brandt, has already been gently prodding Washington to remove its poison gas stocks from West Germany. Where to?

Richard Scott concludes his article on a chilling note:

> There is some suggestion here that Mr Nixon is wondering whether the United Kingdom, which has been compliant about US nuclear submarines with base facilities in Scotland, might be equally co-operative in storage for the nerve gas now in West Germany.

Was the United Kingdom co-operative? Should we have been asked?

The latest story of hazards to arise from involvement with nerve gas weapons appeared in *The Guardian* on 7 May 1979:

> The US Army, after months of indecision, announced last week that it would move 896 nerve gas bombs from an arsenal on the outskirts of Denver to a depot in the Utah desert . . .
>
> Senator Gary Hart (Democrat, Columbia), a member of the Senate Armed Services Committee, joined Utah's Governor Scott Matheson in denouncing the army's decision . . . The army agreed to delay any move for thirty days.
>
> The bombs – theoretically capable of killing 140 billion people, 32 times the world's population – are the remnants of a once vast stockpile of chemical and biological weapons . . . The nerve gas bombs were kept as a deterrent because the Soviet Union still had similar weapons.

The Governor of Utah made a valid point when he said: 'Health and safety should be considered first over national security, but it never has been.'

The army proposed to pack the nerve gas bombs into planes and transfer them over a three week period. The Governor continued:

> Just one bomb is enough to annihilate the entire world. The planes carrying the bombs from Denver would pass within 55 miles of Salt Lake City . . . The deteriorating condition of the bombs means they will eventually be subject to large scale leaks that Tooele army depot, their intended destination, is incapable of coping with.

Curiously enough potential hazard of modern warfare is highlighted by a report on the same page of *The Guardian* which says that the US Army has a large scale drugs problem on its hands; the equivalent of two divisions of American troops in Europe are permanently incapacitated by hard drug addictions. Let us hope that they are not in charge of chemical weapons.

The serious question raised by Utah's Governor Matheson about health and safety is debated in a book called *Surviving Doomsday* by C. Bruce Sibley (published by Shaw & Sons Ltd in 1977). The author considers all the known forms of modern weaponry from the point of view of the civilian. He begins the section on biological warfare (p.44) with this statement:

> The idea of killing thousands to millions of people with nuclear weapons or gas is totally abhorrent to any civilised being, and yet there is still one other form of mass extermination which conjures up perhaps even greater revulsion – I refer to biological warfare.

His message is clear. There is no effort being made to protect the civilian population of Britain from chemical and biological warfare. And there are no plans to provide such protection.

7

Official Policy and Public Protest

In May 1968, the International Conference on Human Rights held at Teheran unanimously adopted a resolution (XXIII) which condemned the use of chemical and biological means of warfare, including napalm. Representatives of 91 nations assented. At the request of the United Nations General Assembly, Secretary General U Thant convened a panel of fourteen experts to prepare a report on CBW, and on the basis of this report in 1969, made three very specific recommendations to governments:

1. to renew the appeal to all states to accede to the Geneva protocol of 1925
2. to make a clear affirmation that the prohibition contained in the Geneva protocol applies to the use in war of all chemical, bacteriological and biological agents (including tear gas and other harassing agents) which now exist or which may be developed in the future
3. to call upon all countries to reach agreement to halt the development, production and stockpiling of all chemical and biological agents for purposes of war and to achieve their elimination from the arsenal of weapons.

The fact that the United States had attacked Vietnam without a declaration of war was used as an excuse for employing techniques which were not permissible under international laws relating to warfare.

The CBW scientists had had their hey-day in the 1950s and 1960s, with almost unlimited budgets, an atmosphere of intense anti-communism in the United States and a Cold War in which paranoia reigned. The secrecy in which the research and development of CBW weapons could be conducted was almost total.

However, by the mid 1960s a change had begun to take place. The CND movement in Britain had impressed many people by its sincerity, and by the time that details of the Vietnam war began to emerge, a feeling of horror and disgust with sophisticated weaponry was developing.

The official excuses being used by the US during this period were:

1. Plants and crops are not covered by the Geneva protocol and therefore defoliation and crop destruction are admissible.
2. The US is not officially at war with Vietnam and the protocol only covers 'use of weapons in war'.
3. The gases being used are not poisonous, and therefore are not covered by the Geneva protocol.

In answer to questions put to the US Defence Department by the Senate Armed Services Committee, Cyrus Vance said: 'We are making use of arsenicals and cyanides in the southern part of Vietnam but not yet in the north.' (November 1965)

Both these forms of gas are poisonous, and when the news broke in Britain of the use of gas in Vietnam in March 1965, Michael Stewart, the then Foreign Secretary, was in Washington. He received the following telegram:

> Urge you convey US government horror indignation aroused parliament and country at use by US forces in Vietnam of gas and napalm, and at threat by US ambassador at Saigon of unlimited extension of war.

It was signed on behalf of a large number of MPs by Philip Noel-Baker, Arthur Blenkinsop, Tom Driberg, John Mendelson, Michael Foot and Sydney Silverman (*The Times*, 23 March 1965). At the same time a motion was tabled in the House of Commons:

> That this House deplores the use of napalm and gas by US forces in Vietnam.

It gathered 104 signatures before it was withdrawn. On his return from Washington, Michael Stewart said 'Britain wholly supports American action in Vietnam' (*The Times*, 25 March 1965).

After pressure in the House a delegation of MPs was allowed

to visit Porton in 1965, but many laboratories were not visited, and not much official information was forthcoming.

On 3 December 1965 *Peace News* reported the existence of Nancekuke as a poison gas station. No-one took any notice of this disclosure, and it was not until 1968 that our anti-CBW group was formed.

The gradual realisation of the United States' attitude to CBW during 1967-68 had affected many people in Britain, and when I wrote to *The Observer* in April 1968, with the object of assessing the amount of public concern about CBW, there was a tremendous response.

Our main objective was to provide informed and responsible support for those scientists and politicians who had been concerned about CBW for a number of years, and one of the main needs was for comprehensive international treaties to control the development and use of CBW.

The chief agency for pressing such international agreements has been the Pugwash committee, a group of eminent scientists from all over the world who were called together by Bertrand Russell.

The first occasion when Soviet scientists joined a discussion of modern weaponry was at a conference organised by a group called the Association of Parliamentarians for World Government, with headquarters in London. This conference took place in London in August 1955.

The conference set up three commissions to study the following subjects:

1. the assessment of the consequences of nuclear weapons, and nuclear power development (Joseph Rotblat as convener)
2. problems of disarmament (Peter Hodgson)
3. social responsibility of scientists (Jacob Bronowski).

The first international conference of scientists was called by Bertrand Russell. As a result of a broadcast he made called 'Man's Peril' on 23 December 1954, and of the publication of a manifesto which received tremendous press and media coverage, support came pouring in from all over the world. The manifesto was intended to be signed by scientists from various countries (and was signed by Einstein two days before his death).

Help came from Cyrus Eaton, a Cleveland industrialist, who offered to finance the conference at Pugwash, Nova Scotia. This conference took place in July 1957; and Pugwash, the little fishing village in Nova Scotia where Cyrus Eaton was born, gave its name to the most influential peace-seeking group of scientists in the world.

The fifth Pugwash conference, in August 1959, was concerned with chemical and biological weapons, though up to this date not enough information had been available for any authoritative assessment to be made. The 26 participants represented eight countries, and the disciplines involved included chemistry, biochemistry, plant biology, microbiology, virology, epideiology, genetics, molecular biology, radiobiology, and a meteorologist, for the purpose of assessing the factors involved in the delivery of these weapons.

Again Cyrus Eaton supported the conference. A statement was prepared and eventually unanimously adopted which was an erudite assessment of the dangers of CBW. Pugwash study groups all over the world have been working on the subject ever since, and have been instrumental in procuring conferences disseminating information, provoking debate and striving to procure treaties limiting or banning chemical and biological weaponry and arms control generally.

The Russell-Einstein manifesto, drafted in 1954, begins:

> In the tragic situation which confronts humanity, we feel that scientists should assemble in conference to appraise the perils that have arisen as a result of the development of weapons of mass destruction, and to discuss a resolution in the spirit of the appended draft . . . We shall try to say no single word which should appeal to one group rather than to another. All equally are in peril, and if the peril is understood, there is hope that we may collectively try to avert it.
>
> We have to learn to think in a new way. We have to learn to ask ourselves, not what steps can be taken to give military victory to whatever group we prefer, for there no longer are such steps; the question we have to ask ourselves is: what steps can be taken to prevent a military contest of which the issue must be disastrous to

all parties... There lies before us, if we choose, continual progress in happiness, knowledge and wisdom. Shall we, instead, choose death because we cannot forget our quarrels. We appeal, as human beings, to human beings: remember your humanity and forget the rest. If you can do so, the way lies open to a new paradise; if you cannot, there lies before you the risk of universal death.

The Resolution

We invite this congress, and through it the scientists of the world and the general public, to subscribe to the following resolution:

> In view of the fact that in any future world war nuclear weapons will certainly be employed, and that such weapons threaten the continued existence of mankind, we urge the governments of the world to realise, and to acknowledge publicly, that their purpose cannot be furthered by a world war, and we urge them, consequently, to find peaceful means for the settlement of all matters of dispute between them.

It was signed by Professor Max Born, Professor P.W. Bridgman, Professor Albert Einstein, Professor L. Infield, Professor J.F. Joliot-Curie, Professor H.J. Muller, Professor Linus Pauling, Professor C.F. Powell, Professor J. Rotblat, Bertrand Russell and Professor Hideki Yukawa, all Nobel Prize winners except Rotblat, Russell, Einstein and Infield.

No nation can develop either chemical or biological weapons without the cooperation of doctors; Dr Gordon Smith of Porton declared that he could keep his staff only if their work was devoted to defence. How he convinced himself or them of this is not clear. How does anyone draw a definitive line between defensive and offensive research in such a field?

The protests of doctors against such work have been dignified and ethically becoming to a professional body, but might perhaps be seen by future generations as being too restrained. To quote from an editorial article from *GP*, 12 June 1970:

> At least in the case of CBW, however, there is something that could be done by doctors... What matters is that CBW affords doctors a unique opportunity to influence, however slightly, the course of events. A firm attitude to CBW on the part of the medical profession, if possible on an international basis, might by a chain reaction increase the chances of these types of arms control... All doctors subscribe to the spirit, if not the letter, of the Hippocratic oath. What practical measures could be taken?... Bodies like the

> BMA could make known publicly and often, their abhorrence of CBW . . . No head of a university should sign the Official Secrets Act . . . authorities which grant medical qualifications could do so on condition that candidates promised not to engage on research on CBW . . . Licensing bodies such as the GMC . . . could, after due warning, withdraw recognition from medically qualified people engaged in such activities.

These measures were not taken, of course, but there had been a conference in London on 25 November 1967 organised by the Conflict Research Society and the Medical Association for the Prevention of War, reported in the *Lancet* of 9 December 1967. Dr Norman MacDonald writes:

> Medical ethics in the past have been mainly concerned with relations between a doctor and his patient, or between himself and his colleagues. They had been generally recognised as serving a useful purpose, but in Nazi Germany the medical ethic as it concerned the patient soon crumbled under the weight of extreme nationalism . . . The immediate issue was whether a doctor's loyalty to a nation state overrode his responsibility to humanity as a whole. Clearly, the problem could not be resolved within the simple context of patriotism when the implications for other people were so profound . . . Each country still pursued its 'national interest' in its own way and this could prove disastrous for science and medicine . . . Speakers suggested that hope for progress lay in expanding activity at the supranational level (UNESCO and WHO). At the same time secrecy in medical research work should be resolutely opposed, and urgent attention given to the ethical implications of modern scientific developments.

On 2 March 1968 the *Lancet* carried a report on the Bernal Peace Library conference in London.

The *Lancet* article said:

> Discussing the ethical implications of biological warfare for the medical profession, Dr V.W. Sidel (Boston) held that the physician not only should refuse to participate in activities which he feels are destructive to his role as healer, but also must actively protest against the development, production and use of biological weapons. Failure to do so represented complicity. Apathy on the part of the medical profession was one of the greatest dangers.

Dr John Humphrey suggested that 'much would be gained by declaring all work at the MRE Porton declassified for a trial period of five years . . . During the trial period at least part of the MRE should be devoted to collaboration with the World Health Organisation.'

Elinor Langer (New York) said: 'Vietnam gives a glimpse of the possibilities and doctors cannot evade the challenge.' Again the *Lancet* (4 May 1968) carried a contribution from Dr V.W. Sidel stressing the moral and ethical responsibilities of doctors with regard to CBW. Such widespread attitudes in the medical profession should be more widely recognised.

A scientist who worked at Porton for a few months said that they were repeatedly pressed to keep the facts of their work (on nerve gas in his case) from the British people. There were prearranged information leaks to Russia almost monthly to impress them with our expertise. (In fact, he maintained that therein lies the most important form of defence.)

There are many other organisations dedicated to anti-CBW aims, but two must be mentioned in particular.

A group of scientists concerned with education started the British Society for Social Responsibility in Science (BSSRS), to encourage and promote awareness of how scientific workers can be used in our society, to form groups in schools, universities and colleges, and to make themselves heard in decisions of a scientific nature made by politicians.

The Stockholm International Peace Research Institute (SIPRI) is foremost in the field of weapons study and research into problems of conflict, particularly disarmament and arms regulation. It was established in 1966 to commemorate Sweden's 150 years of unbroken peace. The Institute is financed by the Swedish parliament, and the staff, governors and scientific council are international. The SIPRI publications are renowned throughout the world for their scientific integrity, objectivity and accuracy.

The depth of involvement of Britain in the offensive military research programme of the United States was gradually emerging as the British anti-CBW campaign grew and our knowledge of the whole picture became more accurate. Every person to whom I have spoken who has worked actively in the British CBW programme admits freely that there were American officers and scientists at Porton and Nancekuke much of the time, and Britain's quadripartite agreement on CBW allowed all information gained by research in Britain to be immediately available to the USA, Canada and Australia.

The attempt made to meet Congressman Richard D. McCarthy (Democrat, New York) at the House of Commons, so that the British and American anti-CBW campaigns might be coordinated, was mysteriously sabotaged.

The Congressman was coming to London in March 1970, and I suggested to a group of MPs who were concerned about CBW (which included Michael Foot) that it might be most valuable to meet Richard McCarthy at the House of Commons. This was arranged, and Richard McCarthy appeared to be delighted.

Several days before the appointment I received a cable from Washington, signed Richard D. McCarthy, saying that he could not come over, but would we make another date to meet in about ten weeks. Naturally I telephoned everyone else concerned (except one) cancelling the arrangement. One woman turned up at the House of Commons at the appointed time, as I had forgotten to notify her. Sybil Cookson of the Women's International League for Peace and Freedom was the only person to greet Congressman McCarthy, who had been greatly looking forward to the meeting and could not understand what had happened; he had not sent the cable cancelling the appointment.

She rang me up demanding to know why I had let him down, but when I explained about the cable it was too late – we did not know where Mr McCarthy was staying.

I heard later that he was much hated by the US army and the Defence Department, and that certain people in the Nixon administration had sworn to get him out of Congress: and in fact he did lose his seat.

I wrote to him in October of 1976, having found his address through the American embassy – 761 Crescent Avenue, Buffalo, New York. I waited for a reply but eventually my air mail letter came back to me marked 'Please forward new address' in handwriting, and then, stamped in red 'Returned to sender. Moved. Not forwardable.'

Another most disturbing aspect of my position in the anti-CBW campaign began to manifest itself in the early spring of 1970. I first realised that my mail was being opened when I received letters from the West German Union of Students, the VDS. They wrote asking for help with their campaign against CBW research in Germany, and said that they were sending me a copy of a magazine called *Konkret* containing an article about stocks of American nerve gas weapons in Germany, and also about the use of German troops in mock nerve gas battles (with photographs). This would have been very important evidence of the Americans using German troops in this way. However, the envelope arrived with GPO sticky tape all round it – 'Found open or damaged and officially secured' – and empty. I wrote and told the VDS and was promised a second copy of *Konkret*. It never arrived. (Can someone supply me with a copy, please?)

From early in 1970 almost every large envelope or package arrived 'damaged', bearing the all too familiar GPO sticky tape. I discovered later that an ecology magazine from Japan had been despatched to me in July 1970; yet another non-arrival.

When I wrote an article on nerve gas victims for *Sogat Journal*, several copies were posted to me from London on 26 March 1970. It had GPO tape all round it – and contained seven letters for other people living in the same Devon village.

The final blow was when a photographer came to take pictures of me and the children for an article that was to appear in *Nova* magazine. She went off promising sheets of proofs as soon as they came out. The photographs were posted on 15 April but were never found. I protested to the GPO and eventually two inspectors came from Bristol to examine my damaged envelopes and take all the particulars. On 13 July I received an official letter of apology.

I was told on many occasions by journalists that my telephone was tapped – it certainly behaved in some extraordinary ways – but how can one have proof?

As early as May 1968 large groups of scientists in the United States and Australia had produced petitions calling for the renunciation of CBW. 680 Australian scientists organised meetings and debates, and signed a petition. We do not know of any CBW research, testing, dumping or stockpiling in Australia, though there is an official testing site (at Innisfail) in Queensland, and Britain has quadripartite agreement on CBW to share all information with the USA, Canada and Australia.

A large group of professional men in the United States, headed by 22 scientists and doctors (including seven Nobel Prize winners) presented a petition against CBW to President Johnson; this petition had the written backing of 5000 US scientists and 129 members of the National Academy of Sciences.

The British Council of Churches in conjunction with the Society of Friends (Quakers) and the United Nations Association brought out a pamphlet entitled *'The Geneva protocol and CS gas'*, reiterating the plea to the British government to support the Geneva protocol.

In June 1968 21 British scientists (including eight Nobel prize winners) wrote to Harold Wilson (the then Prime Minister) calling for the publication of all work carried out at Porton, and asking that the work be declassified and, as it was purported to be defensive and prophylactic research, that it be transferred to the aegis of the Medical Research Council.

Harold Wilson replied on 28 June 1968 that 'it would be difficult to move responsibility for the establishment away from the Ministry of Defence'.

In his reply Wilson explained that some measure of secrecy was essential so as not to reveal the country's preparedness and some of the agents on which we were working. There is no mention here of 'purely defensive work'.

One most emotive aspect of CBW research is the use made of animals; apparently Porton scientists are more apprehensive about the anti-vivisection protestors than about any others. The prospect of inflicting unimaginable suffering on live animals for the purposes of medical research is disquieting enough, but the use of hundreds of thousands of live animals to perfect methods of mass slaughter is utterly repugnant.

I wrote to Harold Wilson, James Callaghan, Denis Healey

and to the director of Porton about various aspects of CBW, but never had an honest or intelligent reply.

This was in marked contrast to letters I had from Anthony Wedgwood Benn. He answered not only my specific questions, but also referred to the implicit philosophical issues raised by our campaign. For example, he wrote:

> If protest and political action become totally alienated, protest would become evanescent, and government uninspired, because it would not connect with the conscience of the people.

That sentence should be prominently displayed in the House of Commons.

The anti-CBW campaign was not a structured, carefully planned strategy for ending CBW in Britain. It was a haphazard and pragmatic use of every piece of information that we could obtain.

What I learned through it was that there were many people in Britain – and in other parts of the world – who still cared enough to fight.

8

Open Day at Nancekuke

It was a fine windy day in October 1970 when the press was allowed to visit Nancekuke. I was there by courtesy of *Peace News*. Most of the journalists had travelled down on the London train to Camborne, and had been driven to a hotel as an assembly point, before scaling the heights of Portreath and being admitted *en masse* by the security guards.

I had been interviewed by a battery of local and national BBC radio and television reporters the previous evening, and had spent the night locally.

The taxi driver who took me to Nancekuke was a young Cornishman, who told me that the people of Portreath hated and feared Nancekuke, but, as there was so much unemployment in Cornwall, they dared not offend the Ministry of Defence whose presence brought some prosperity to a very poor area.

He was very aware of the possibility of accidents or sabotage, and was cynical about the possibility of protection or compensation for local people if anything did go wrong. He told me stories of people who claimed to have suffered mysterious chest ailments and nervous disorders; he mentioned the dying seals, and said that skin divers had disappeared off that coast with no explanation. There were tales of strangely deformed plants and vegetables occurring around the area.

All this added up to a picture of fear and speculation very different from anything which the press had been told by Cornish councillors, doctors and other local officials.

When we arrived at the gates of Nancekuke my heart was like lead. The security guards looked at my press card and regarded me coldly. We were then directed to an assembly point in the central administrative block where it was most reassuring to see so many journalists, many of whom I had met before.

The hall was lined with plaster figures clothed in gas masks and protective suits of various brands. Security men, plain clothes police and civil servants were there in ranks, wearing labels announcing their roles – if not their names. We were told that we were to be escorted around in small groups, accompanied by Porton security men, and transported in vans.

It is difficult to convey the sordid quality of the buildings. The obviously new whitewash which covered every surface scarcely concealed the shabby ugliness of the buildings, and the intermittent baying of the guard dogs, shut up for that day, contrasted strongly with the wheeling seagulls and glimpses of the beautiful Cornish coast.

The worst place of all was the nerve gas plant. It was housed in a high, bleak building, and its internal mechanical complexity was completely incomprehensible. I have experienced steel factories and coal mines, but this was something different.

When the Director, Neville Gadsby, arrived, I asked him questions about the protection of civilians, the danger of attracting attack by our involvement with the US offensive posture on CBW, the risks to the workers involved, and about the ethics of producing gas when Britain was signatory to the Geneva protocol. Gadsby made it very clear that he was not going to answer any such questions. So I said, 'Mr Gadsby, can you tell me in what capacity you are here?' He replied angrily that he was present 'purely and simply as a technologist'. As he was departing he shouted, 'I resent the presence of that tape recorder!' It was not my manner, but the content of my questions, which caused his outburst.

Later during the tour, an angry scientist shouted at me: 'We see more of you on television than anyone else. We're sick of your face and your nonsense and we can't answer your crazy allegations.' I pointed out that it was not me who wielded the Official Secrets Act which imposed silence on them. I told him that during our campaign we had repeatedly asked for an open debate and that part of our complaint against the Ministry of Defence was that no debate ever took place.

The isolation and anonymity of scientists working at such places seemed to me to be most undesirable, and their separation from mainstream society had obviously created a secretive and distorted community. Their 'inside' activity and conversation, never contradicted or challenged, could not withstand exposure from the 'outside', even less from analytical debate with non-scientists or military personnel with experience in other fields.

Another example of this came when I asked a technician in the CS production plant if he had ever seen the effects of CS on a child. He turned and hurried away.

Three workmen gave a very different impression. They waved and shouted encouragingly, possibly because they knew I had fought for compensation for their workmates who had been disabled. I hope that is how they saw it.

Later I was shown the doorway and steps leading down into the nerve gas bunker, with the guard-rabbit in its air filtration cage, and was urged to have a look at the two 50-gallon drums of nerve gas inside. It was not a sight I could contemplate with equanimity, and I refused. 'Surely you're not afraid of being gassed?', I was asked. But how could I possibly convey to such men what I saw and felt?

The visit to the medical block provided another shock. The medical officer at Nancekuke had been changed since Tom Griffiths's case had appeared in the press, and the doctor to whom I spoke had never heard of him. He talked a little about cholinesterase inhibition, seeming never to have read any of the major papers on nerve gas poisoning. He admitted that he did not know of the cases of alleged poisoning at Nancekuke, and was amazed at the news.

Moving on from that to a lecture on antidotes to nerve gas was more like *Alice Through the Looking Glass* than any normal human experience. We were shown automatic hypodermics, fitted to anti-CBW suits, that shot atropine into the thigh of the combatant engaged in a gas battle. As atropine is a deadly drug the dose must be calculated very carefully otherwise it might kill the patient. When I asked about the dangers involved in its use the lecturer appeared to be nonplussed, and would only say that it had all been carefully calculated. He briefly described other antidotes without giving any details, or any indication of the difficulties or dangers inherent in using these substances.

To convey the irresponsibility of this lecture given, after all, to a group who were mostly technical and scientific journalists, I must refer to chapter 3 of a SIPRI monograph on *Medical Protection Against Chemical Warfare Agents* (1976).

> The most important therapeutic measure against organophosphate poisoning is the injection of atropine as a pharmacodynamic antagonist of acetyl choline. Although atropine has only a symptomatic antidotal effect – it does not influence the root of the intoxication, the inhibition of the enzyme – it is fast and reliable in action, and is effective in combating cramp and spasms of the bronchi and glottis. It is thus a valuable means of gaining the time necessary for applying the additional therapeutic measures, such as artificial respiration and the injection of reactivating antidotes.

In a later section of the same chapter Professor Erdman says:

> In contrast to atropine, which must be given in very high doses very rapidly after organophosphate intoxication, and then at regular intervals for many days or even weeks, pyridinium oximes must be administered in limited doses and only over a limited period of time . . . This does not mean that oxime therapy is always successful, and with some cases of organophosphate poisoning oximes will have very little, if any, effect.

Unfortunately I did not have such valuable documentary evidence available in 1970, and had only been told that the sanguine claims of antidotes or cures for nerve gas poisoning were seriously misleading.

However, I did ask the lecturer what provisions there were for the treatment of civilians in case of attack, and how such antidotes could possibly be administered in a civil situation; but he knew nothing of therapy for civilians.

Later a friend from Cornwall wrote to Cornwall's Medical Officer for Health, and then to the Ministry, asking where she should apply for gas masks, protective suits and antidotes against nerve gas attacks for herself and her family. There was no reply. So much for the claim that 'it is all for our defence'.

Even the combatants would not be protected adequately. A

report in the *Daily Telegraph* in June 1976 quoted the Swedish (SIPRI) document as saying:

> Clothing capable of giving full bodily protection to the skin and to the respiratory system is so cumbersome that soldiers wearing it would be brought to the point of military uselessness . . . In a vapour cloud the concentration of nerve agent may be high and there is a danger that the charcoal filters in the [NATO] gas masks could become saturated, rendering the masks useless . . . In war it is unlikely that medical facilities would be able to cope with the vast number of casualties.

After lunch – ruined for me by all that we had seen – we returned to the main reception hall (still lined by the forbidding plaster figures) and were addressed by various officials.

The content of the speeches was minimal. The art of evading all the relevant and important facts, of never entering into debate on any significant level, was effortlessly maintained. Neville Gadsby spoke last, then invited questions.

The science correspondent on *The Times* asked about the effect of any toxic waste escaping into the sea. Gadsby said that if something unpleasant escaped, the fish would swim away. Somehow this answer did not strike the note of technological expertise that we had been led to expect.

Neville Gadsby's statement on the after-effects of exposure to organophosphorus compounds was equivocal. He said that there was no incontrovertible evidence that sublethal doses of nerve gas produce long-term or delayed effects on anything other than chickens. (The only reported experiments from Porton were conducted on chickens.)

The annual budget for Nancekuke, we learned, was £330,000, which supported a staff of 175.

One scientific journalist present suggested that genetic engineering formed a part of the work at Nancekuke. The response to this was non-committal. (In a subsequent article the *Sunday Times* journalist concluded that the crucial point about Nancekuke was its research capabilities. '. . . under the quadripartite agreement . . . chemical warfare is divided: Nancekuke for research and development, Canada and Australia for testing, and America for production'.)

By the time our visit was ending, two men from Porton were arguing about the ethics of publishing toxicity data of chemicals to be used against civilians, the ethics of using such chemicals in civilian situations, and the role of the ruling political party in such matters.

To promote open and informed debate about CBW had always been a central aim of our campaign; was this a beginning?

As we left the gates of Nancekuke a journalist asked me what I had learned during the visit. The experience had had such a profound effect that I could not tell him; it was worse than I could have imagined, but the fact that we had been allowed in at all was a major breakthrough.

Looking back, that day was the beginning of the end for Nancekuke's role as a production and development plant for the Ministry of Defence. From then plans were made to close the plant.

The announcement came in March 1976 that Nancekuke *was* to close, but by that time the views expressed in the press were mostly concerned with unemployment and its ramifications.

In 1979, the proposal to convert Nancekuke to a NATO radar station was announced. It coincided with the visit of 22 scientists and diplomats, arranged by the Foreign Office. The purpose of this visit was to prove to an international group of scientists and UN officials that inspection and verification of the demolition of chemical plant was feasible, and that Britain could lead the way in this field of disarmament; and to press for a total ban on the production and stockpiling of chemical weapons.

Places like Nancekuke might not exist if the scientists working there had been trained under a less selective and specialised educational policy. If, instead, children were taught to analyse and criticise what their roles in life were to be, and if scientifically gifted children were taught the humanities, civics and sociology, they might have a more balanced outlook.

I also believe that religious leaders should involve themselves far more in areas of public morality and safety, such as that of CBW; there are bishops in this country, with establishments like Porton or Nancekuke in their diocese, who know nothing of the work that is done in such places. When asked, they say it is nothing to do with them. Some involve themselves in various aspects of socially responsible work and comment, and the Quakers have been outspoken in their condemnation of modern weaponry, but other churches feel it is safer not to know.

The former Bishop of Crediton, Wilfred Westall, when asked to bless a nuclear submarine, wrote back that he would gladly curse its existence.

One of the saddest moments during the day at Nancekuke was when I was alone for a moment, and could stand and gaze at the cliffs and sea and could remember what I used to feel about this part of Cornwall. Now it was Nancekuke. Nerve gas. CS. Dying seals.

A friend once sent me a Christmas card that he had made. It depicted a man in a gas mask standing on a cliff shouting through a megaphone 'I'm sorry, I'm sorry, I'm sorry . . .' across a plain filled with dead and dying people and animals. 'I'm sorry . . .'

9

Implications of CBW

The Geneva protocol of 1925 was a restatement of the prohibition on the use of poisonous gases previously laid down by the Versailles and Washington treaties of 1919 and 1922 respectively; a ban on bacteriological weapons was added at the suggestion of Poland.

Before the second world war many countries ratified the protocol including all the great powers except the US and Japan.

During the Korean war the Soviet Union introduced a draft resolution in the Security Council of the UN urging all members to ratify the protocol, but the US wished to implement a disarmament agreement with effective safeguards. On 26 June 1952, the Soviet resolution was rejected by a vote of 1 to 0 with ten abstentions, including the US, UK and France. *(Arms Control and Disarmament Agreements,* US Arms Control and Disarmament Agency, 1975).

When the communist countries criticised the US for its use of gas and herbicides in Vietnam in 1966, the Geneva protocol was quoted by Hungary in the UN General Assembly, but the US denied that it applied to 'non-toxic gases and herbicides'.

On 11 August 1970 Secretary of State Rogers presented a report to President Nixon recommending that the protocol be ratified, with a reservation of the right to retaliate with gas if an enemy state, or its allies, violated the protocol, and also reaffirming the right to use riot control agents and herbicides.

On 22 January 1975 President Ford ratified the Geneva protocol and the Biological Weapons Convention.

Under the terms of the convention on biological weapons, the parties undertake not to develop, produce, stockpile or acquire biological agents or 'toxins' of types and in quantities that have no justification for prophylactic, protective or other uses, as well as weapons and means of delivery. All such material to be destroyed within nine months of the convention's entry into force.

The news that the CIA retained a stock of cobra venom and guns for delivering the toxin came to light in the aftermath of the Watergate scandal, and the CIA was ordered to destroy all stocks at once.

The question of a ban on all chemical weapons has been under discussion within the United Nations for the last twenty years, and involves highly complex issues. The general headings under which the debate takes place are as follows:

1. the scope of prohibition
2. the activities which should be banned
3. the agents that should be subject to such prohibition
4. the way in which compliance to the convention should be verified.

This last point appears to present the greatest problems, and verification techniques are obviously related to the substances and activities involved; that is why the inspection of Nancekuke was of such significance.

The USSR still persists in its disapproval of international verification procedures, while the Western states continue to hold that international on-site inspection should be part of the measures agreed.

Let us not forget that the binary nerve gas weapons, which combine on impact two non-lethal chemical agents to form a lethal nerve gas, are still with us; and that the control of such weapons is in our hands. In the last analysis all we can do is to hope that by continuing the effort to obtain rational and responsible international agreements, plus effective verification systems on weaponry, such efforts will succeed.

The value of the British anti-CBW campaign has been its success in bringing the issues of CBW into the open. The media coverage of the subject has meant that large numbers of people now know that nerve gas is a 'conventional' weapon, and that there really were stocks of bubonic plague bacillus ready for use as weapons. For the British Foreign Office to bring the struggle for an international ban on biological weapons to a successful conclusion such publicity was necessary.

The need for incessant public protest about the horrific aspects of modern technology is very important. As Anthony Wedgwood Benn said, speaking at the inaugural meeting of the Science, Technology and Society Association in March 1979:

> It is only quite recently that people have begun to express concern that there may be a price to be paid for technical development in respect of our prospects for the democratic control of our society, and our personal freedom within it.
>
> The most obvious example lies in the military field, where technologies, financed entirely by public expenditure at the behest of governments, have created huge armed forces all of which operate under the military discipline of the various Chiefs of Staffs throughout the world, and are thus responsible for the application of defence policy.

Another aspect of weaponry is that it earns money for Britain. There has been much debate recently about the morality of selling sophisticated weaponry and supplying spare parts to questionable regimes throughout the world. The usual arguments in favour are 'if we didn't supply them somebody else would', 'it makes money' and 'it would create enormous unemployment if we stopped'. Such arguments are pathetic when placed against the threats which modern weaponry present.

The Director of Porton, when addressing a meeting of Civil Defence officers in May 1979, said that Britain exports protective clothing against nerve gas not only to America, but also to the Arab states. None is available to British civilians.

Political and sociological analysis of the position of the armed forces in modern society is vital, and so is the scientist's view of the politician; Michael Kenward, in *New Scientist* of 29 March 1979, wrote: 'the role of science must become a more important issue than crowd control at football matches or potholes in country roads'. He believes that the Energy Secretary should concern himself with the democratic control of science and technology.

Shirley Williams, then the Minister for Education, said:

'Scientists themselves, whose profession is so often silent, need to explain more of what they are doing.' But Mr Kenward protests:

> It is all very well for politicians, who have suddenly discovered that science has social implications . . . to rail on at scientists for keeping them in the dark, but is it any wonder that scientists have not acquired the habit of talking to politicians when the latter previously showed less than minimal interest in things scientific?. . .
>
> If politicians and the public – that great unknown referred to by both Benn and Williams – really want to hear from scientists then they should listen all the time, not just in an election year or when it is expedient to do so.

This is not always as easy as it sounds. Anthony Tucker writing in *The Guardian* in the same week (27 March 1979) reported that an international conference on genetic engineering is being criticised by scientists for its secrecy. He said:

> The conference, organised jointly by the Royal Society and by the Committee on Genetic Engineering Experimentation (COGENE) of the International Council of Scientific Unions is closed to the press, although a press conference to announce its conclusions is planned by the Royal Society.

Three nominated members of the British Association of Science Writers were to be allowed in to the meeting, 'although its proceedings will remain "absolutely private" until they are published in a few months' time . . . Closed scientific meetings are commonplace, especially where free discussion is essential but, in an area of high sensitivity, secrecy of this kind is bound to arouse suspicions.'

The meeting was convened in Wye by the European Molecular Biology Association, and in part appeared to wish to promote the idea that the dangers of genetic engineering have been overplayed, and that compulsory controls could be harmful. In reply to this, union members of Britain's Genetic Manipulation Advisory Group (GMAG) said:

> The issue was not simply one of adequate control of a potentially hazardous technology capable of creating organisms with characteristics which do not occur in nature, but of public participation in scientific and technological decision-making.

The pressure for greater freedom from compulsory safety measures comes from industry, and the GMAG committee – an advisory committee with representatives of all those involved, including laymen – has the power to assign security priorities or reject experiments altogether, and must be recognised as a unique advance in public participation in science.

Unfortunately the EEC draft guidelines will give fewer controls, and greater latitude to industry. British pressure for stringent controls was not represented adequately at the Wye conference and, as Anthony Tucker said:

> Since the potential applications of genetic engineering appear to lie first in production of hormones and other natural substances used in medicine and later in the creation of biologically based chemical systems with an enormous potential range, the issues are extremely important.

A government announcement made on 15 February 1979 said that Porton Down was to be divided. Control of part of the Microbiological Research Establishment is to be handed over to the Public Health Laboratory Service from 1 April 1979. In an article from *The Guardian* (15 February 1979) part of the work was described by David Ennals: 'Current projects included production of various vaccines and work on genetic engineering, and the centre should be known as the Centre of Applied Microbiology and Research.'

Later in the same article Patrick Jenkin (the Shadow Social Services Secretary) said 'The biggest and most exciting potential for Porton is in industrial microbiology. Security at Porton is excellent, and it should be an ideal centre for work on dangerous viruses, microbiological studies and genetic engineering.'

The position of the scientists in the centre of all these fields is a delicate and responsible one, requiring a proper understanding of the social and political implications of their work.

Tony Benn said in *The Guardian* in February 1979:

> Scientists and technologists cannot only inject their social and political values into their decisions at the ballot box. They must inject them directly through their own work, and the choices that they make in their work, even if it involves dissenting on certain occasions, from the discipline of the firms or organisations, public

or private, national or international, from which they draw their incomes.

Helveg Petersen, the Danish Disarmament Minister, speaking at the third Pugwash conference of leading world scientists called for 'a kind of revolution which transcends national frontiers ... where it becomes a task of high priority to change the pattern of actions followed by nations as to war and peace'.

The idea of scientists demanding the right to know to what use their work is to be put, and to have the right to veto such work, is new but, when we consider the weaponry available to the world's military forces, it is essential.

In September 1978 USSR Party Secretary Leonid Brezhnev made a speech to the United Nations, demanding control of 'new weapons, even more awesome than nuclear arms'. The implication was that the arms race between the USSR and the US had reached a point of breakthrough which could present an even greater threat to the survival of the human race.

Victor Zorza, writing of possible developments in weaponry, mentioned lasers and

> the anti-matter weapon, even more remote as a practical possibility, one which would derive from the total conversion of matter into energy, the annihilation of matter, and could yield a destructive power a thousand times greater than present nuclear devices.
>
> Biological weapons might conceivably qualify for the 'more awesome than nuclear' category, but they are now banned by international agreements to which both the United States and the Soviet Union adhere. Some chemical weapons such as the new binary gas might also be regarded as more awesome.

The perfection of weather modification techniques are known to be under scrutiny in the weaponry industry, as are methods of 'environmental warfare'. The latter includes melting polar ice caps, creating hurricanes and artificially inducing earthquakes, as well as blasting 'windows' in the ozone layer in order to let through ultraviolet rays which would incinerate all living things in their path.

The appeal for a comprehensive ban on all such methods of destroying life must be taken seriously, and it is not until the public takes a hand in demanding such a ban that governments are pushed into complying. The fear of losing political power is still greater than that of slipping behind in the race for even more efficient ways of destroying life.

The difficulty experienced by the layman in believing such science fiction horrors has been one of the stumbling blocks to keeping these politically vital subjects in the public eye. However, two incidents in the last few years have helped to rectify this. One was the chemical works disaster at Seveso in Italy; the other was the escape of a smallpox virus at Birmingham University.

In Seveso, near Milan, a Swiss-owned chemical company was manufacturing a substance called trichlorophenol, which is an intermediate for the herbicide 2,4,5-T, apparently without the knowledge of the Italian government or the authorities and residents of Seveso. In July 1976 a safety valve blew and dioxin and trichlorophenol were blown into the sky, falling to earth as a white cloud of ash over Seveso.

As a result of this accident a Vietnamese expert on dioxin poisoning, Professor Tan Than Thut, was asked to advise the Italian government. He had worked in the Viet Duc Hospital, Hanoi, when the Americans were bombarding Vietnam with 64 million litres of defoliant chemicals.

> More than 100 kilograms of dioxin (the contaminant of the herbicide 2,4,5-T) were injected into the South Vietnamese environment, and had affected large areas of forest, and was still detected in soil a decade after the attack.

This report came from Professor Arthur Westing of Windham College, Vermont, USA, speaking at an Institute of Biology meeting in London on 23 September 1976. He went on:

> The lasting loss which would probably take upwards of a century to recover was equivalent to the food requirement of 1.6 million people and involved areas too large and too damaged for systematic reclamation.

Professor Tan Than Thut is quoted as saying, 'for every 1000 people contaminated by 2,4,5-T, 300 die. The deaths begin some months after poisoning and continue for years.'

In Vietnam the number of deaths from cancer of the liver

increased by 500 per cent after the country was bombarded with the defoliant, and 48 in every thousand children were stillborn.

The other accident, which occurred in September 1978, was the escape of a smallpox virus at Professor Henry Bedson's smallpox laboratory at Birmingham University. This caused the death of Janet Parker, a photographer at the University and unleashed a great deal of speculation and concern about the work Professor Bedson was actually doing. The Professor subsequently committed suicide.

Clive Jenkins, general secretary of Janet Parker's union, the Association of Scientific, Technical and Managerial Staffs (ASTMS), claimed that Professor Bedson's smallpox laboratory might have been carrying out unauthorised research that created a new type of smallpox virus (*New Scientist*, 19 October 1978). 'We have the deepest suspicion that Janet Parker did not die of variola major,' he said, 'and we feel that there might have been unauthorised experimentation at Birmingham [University] with other dangerous pathogens or with other recombinant techniques.'

Eventually a spokesperson for Birmingham University told the ASTMS that Janet Parker was infected by variola, but did not specify with which strain.

It is interesting to remember that Birmingham University had had one of the contracts with the Porton Microbiological department in 1968, and that Professor Henry Bedson and Professor Keith Dumbell were working together on hybrid smallpox/cowpox strains which they had created together in the 1960s.

The work of this laboratory, it has been suggested, should be transferred to the Centre of Applied Microbiology and Research at Porton Down.

Another curious happening in 1978 was the mysterious death of Georgy Markov, a Bulgarian broadcaster working for the BBC, who was stabbed in the leg with a poisoned umbrella. Peter Deeley said in the *Observer* (7 January 1979):

> Four months of exhaustive work by detectives and forensic scientists have led only to a red brick wall.
>
> Of three questions – who? why? and how? – two still remain: the identity of the killers and their motive. Answering the third –

how Markov died – has taken the combined work of detectives, metallurgists, pathologists and toxicologists.

The substance deposited in Markov's leg in a minute pellet, made of a metal alloy containing 90 per cent platinum and 10 per cent iridium, was ricin. Ricin is one of the five most toxic materials known, and was the subject of the controversial Ministry of Defence contract at Exeter University's chemistry department, headed by a Professor Rydon, in the 1960s.

Ricin has been of interest to British scientists for many years, and Porton scientists developed a ricin bomb (the W bomb) during the second world war. Professor Rydon worked at Porton then and, at the time of the ricin contract at Exeter, was an advisor to Porton.

Despite British interest in this substance, when the results of the coroner's inquest into Markov's death were announced, the BBC said in a news bulletin: 'Ricin is a highly toxic substance which has been investigated mainly in Russia and Czechoslovakia.'

The Markov case highlighted the fallacy that a Ministry of Defence contract concerning ricin provides the expertise to detect its presence in a victim with any speed, or the ability to provide any antidote, a defence against its use as a chemical warfare agent, as Professor Rydon had claimed in *Chemistry in Britain* (volume 4 number 7, July 1968).

In April 1978 a report was published by the Council for Science and Society, called 'Harmless Weapons'. This was an investigation of the policy with regard to police weapons for riot control, and largely ignored the political issues involved, though it does contain the following conclusion:

> One can only hope that others – and especially parliamentarians – will take the view that the delicate web of the existing social order could ultimately be destroyed merely by continuing the secrecy and lack of information . . . through a drift towards a dangerous reliance by the authorities for control of civil disorder on sophisticated weapons generally assumed to be harmless.
>
> If this conclusion is even remotely right then the sooner we start talking more openly about the techniques by which law and order could come to be safeguarded in the future, and about the criteria and procedures by which decisions will be made, the better for all of us (Paul Sieghart, *New Scientist*, March 1978).

The report does not include any reference to techniques used in Northern Ireland, but it does point out that the expression 'harmless weapon' is a contradiction in terms.

The report stresses that discussion of this subject is vital, and is not taking place.

The British Society for the Social Responsibility in Science (BSSRS) replied to this report by saying that 'with reference to chemical weapons . . . the US army land warfare laboratory (which carries out extensive safety testing) said that "no matter how discreet the use of chemical agents is, there is always an element of risk of developing a lethal concentration".'

The British government struggled to maintain that CS gas was a 'smoke' (see chapter 3) until in February 1979 the Home Office released film through the BBC showing police using cartridges of 'smokeless CS gas'.

The new form of CR riot control gas is still shrouded in secrecy; *Nature* magazine described the published research on CR as 'entirely inadequate'.

Even more worrying were questions asked in the House of Commons on 'psychological techniques' being taught to the police at the Joint Warfare Establishment, Old Sarum, Wiltshire. The name for this area of training is 'psycops', and the establishment works in close collaboration with Fort Bragg in the United States (*The Guardian*, 28 October 1976).

The Guardian quoted a restricted document which describes the Joint Warfare Establishment's work:

> Psycops, in conjunction with other instruments of power, can make important contributions towards achieving national objectives, by changing the attitudes, opinions and behaviour of hostile and unfriendly groups, and by reinforcing those of allied, friendly ones.

Who is to decide who is 'hostile' and who is 'friendly'?

Tom Litterick (Labour MP for Birmingham Selly Oak) tabled a detailed series of questions on this subject for the Home Secretary, Merlyn Rees. He also asked the Ministry of Defence to publish the course syllabus for the establishment, and asked the Northern Ireland Secretary, Roy Mason, how many of his staff have received instruction there.

It is essential, as the Council for Science and Society suggests, that:

> It will not be too much longer before one or other of the Houses of Parliament can find time to discuss this subject . . . The public in general, and those whom it elects to represent it both locally and nationally, may one day be very directly – and perhaps painfully – concerned with the consequences of policy decisions in this field. If that is right, then it and its political representatives should have the power to ascertain what is being done in its name.

But how can we – the people – keep a democracy alive when an official policy of secrecy prevents information on governmental decisions from reaching the electorate?

The Guardian leader (31 March 1979) put the case succinctly:

> The Labour government came to power specifically committed to greater openness about official activities. In future, its manifesto said, public authorities would have to justify withholding information. Last summer's White Paper on official secrecy substantially reneged on that commitment. The Queen's speech last November committed the government to 'strengthen our democracy by providing new opportunities for citizens to take part in the decisions that affect their lives'. Since then we have seen the government front bench showing every indication that it would excise the public right to official information from Mr Clement Freud's now defunct Bill.

The irrationality of the situation is highlighted by the news, reported in the *New Scientist* and *Daily Mirror* of 12 October 1978, that nerve gas patents were freely available to anyone in the Patent Office in Chancery Lane, London.

These patents are in the American section of the Foreign Patent Library, and appear to have been overlooked after the *Sunday Times* revealed the presence of British patents VE and VM in the UK files in 1975. These patents were removed, and retroactive legislation to legalise this action followed.

The *New Scientist* said:

> Anybody wishing to contaminate a small pond may consult this US patent ['Production of toxic organophosphorus compounds']. In it is described an experiment in which the necessary basic non-toxic chemicals are added to a pond of 100,000 gallons. After twenty five

hours, we are told, 'the pond contains 0.2 parts per million and the concentration continues to increase with time'. There are also several recipes for cooking up in a laboratory.

Such obviously dangerous information was freely available to anyone, yet the Ministry of Defence quibbled at telling the British people how much mustard gas is to be stored at Dartmoor National Park army camp (*New Scientist*, 20 March 1979).

Tony Benn has been the one constant Ministerial voice to demand open government and a realistic approach to freedom of information. Writing in *The Guardian* of 10 February 1979 he said:

> If we are driven by new problems to introduce new security measures then we can quickly drift into a situation in which the democratic freedoms are in danger . . . Technology always provides the ways and means to enforce security . . . Could we back into a police state because of high technology? I invite you to consider this as a serious question . . .

The anti-CBW campaign was formed as a reaction to revelations of existing forms of weaponry which had hitherto been seen only in the pages of science fiction; a concept of warfare designed to kill the maximum number of unprotected non-combatants.

There are other forms of weaponry which are just as horrific, and the struggle against all of them must go on. There *is* hope – as long as people have the courage to look at what is happening and to say 'No'.

Bibliography

Hollingshead, M. *The Man Who Turned on the World*, London, Blond & Briggs 1973

Hunter, Donald, *Health in Industry*, Harmondsworth, Penguin 1959

Landry, Ernest, *Nancekuke: A Memory*, Cornwall, the author, 1978

McCarthy, Richard D. *The Ultimate Folly*, London, Gollancz 1970

Nottingham, J. and J. Cookson, *War: A New Perspective*, Newcastle Peace Group, Newcastle University, 1968

Rose, Steven, ed. *CBW (London Conference on CBW)* London, Harrap, 1968

Rotblat, J., *Pugwash: A History of the Conferences on Science and World Affairs*, Czechoslovak Academy of Sciences, 1967

Sibley, C. Bruce, *Surviving Doomsday*, London, Shaw & Sons

Scheflin, A & E. Opton, *The Mind Manipulators*, London, Paddington Press 1978

SIPRI, *Chemical Disarmament*, London, Taylor & Francis 1975

SIPRI, *Delayed Toxic Effects of Chemical Warfare Agents*, London, Taylor & Francis 1975

SIPRI, *Effects of Developments in the Biological and Chemical Sciences on CW Disarmament Negotiations*, London, Taylor & Francis 1974

SIPRI, *Medical Protection Against CW Agents*, London, Taylor & Francis 1976

SIPRI, *Problems of Chemical and Biological Warfare*, London, Taylor & Francis 1971-75, 6 vols.

United Nations Secretary General, *Chemical and Bacteriological Weapons: Report of the UN Secretary General*, 1969

World Health Organisation, *Health Aspects of CBW*, WHO 1969

World Federation of Scientific Workers, *ABC Weapons: Disarmament and the Responsibility of Scientists*, London, WFSW 1971

World Federation of Scientific Workers, *Chemical Weapons Must Be Banned*, London, WFSW 1974

Index

accidents, 78ff.
accidents, smallpox, 109,110
African swine fever, 65
agent orange, 109,110
animal experiments, 9
anthrax, 10,6
anti-CBW
   campaign, 104,114
   group, 8,87
antimatter, 108
arms control and disarmament (UN), 103
arms sales, 105
atropine, 11,32,98
attack, simulated, 71
AUEW, 34,37

Bernal Peace Library, 7
Bidstrup, Dr Patricia, 25,31ff.
binary nerve gas, 104
biological ban, 103
biological weapons, 10
Birmingham smallpox accident, 109,110
botulism, 10
brainwashing, 67
British Society for Social Responsibility in Science, 53,75, 91,112
bubonic plague, 10
BZ, 10,65ff.

Canadian testing ground, 72,73
chemical and biological warfare
   doctors and, 89ff.
   patents, 113,114
   politics and, 101
   research in US, 70ff.
   scientist's role in, 107,108
   Sweden's attitude to research, 9
   teach-in, 8
   WHO report on, 19
   UN on, 85
Chalfont, Lord, 45
chemical agents, transport of, 77
chemical ban, 104
cholera, 10
cholinesterase, 18,31ff.
church, role of leaders, 101
CIA, 12,13,65,67,104
civil defence, 9,72,84,99,100
CN, 10
CND, 86
cobra venom, 104
Cockayne, William, 20ff., 28
Cookson, John, 12,13
CR, 56,57,112
CS, 9,10,11,13,15,43ff.,112
   deaths, 12
   experiments, 51,52
   export, 14
   lethality, 14
   Northern Ireland, 46ff.
   Paris riots, 47

Dartmoor Army Camp, 113,114
delayed effects of CBW agents, 67
DFP, 22
dioxin, 109
disarmament conference, 78
disease, animal, 65
DM, 10
DMT, 10
D notice, 13
doctors and CBW, 89ff.
drugs, space, 69
Dugway testing ground, 74

Edgewood Arsenal, 10,70
effluent from Nancekuke, 77,100
Einstein, Albert, 88
encephalitis, 10,60,61
environmental warfare, 108
Essex University, 16
Exeter University, 7,111
experiments
  animals, 9
  biological weapons, 58
  foetuses, 72
  elderly humans, 63
  humans, 58,61ff.

finances for CBW, US and UK, 59
foetuses, experiments on, 72
Foreign Office, 105
Fort Bragg, 112
Fort Detrick, 72
Fort Gulick, 65

Gadsby, G. N., 97
gas, CS, 9
genetic engineering, 100,106,107
Geneva Protocol, vi,11,13,103
Griffiths, Thomas, 28ff.
Gruinard, 10,60

Haddon, Eric, 11,52,64
harassing agents, 10

herbicide, 2,4,5-T, 109,110
Himsworth committee, 47,49
human rights, International
  Conference on, 85
Hunter, Dr Donald, 20,33,37

ICI, 20
incapacitators, 10,67ff.
Inch, Dr, 16
Institute of Professional and Civil
  Servants, 19
interrogation, 67
Iran, sale of CS to, 57

Joint Warfare Establishment, 112

Kazantzis, Dr, 38

lachrymators, 10
lasers, 108
Leary, Dr Timothy, 68ff.
Lee Det. Insp. Richard, 70
Lohs, K, 19
Long Kesh, 55,56
LSD, 10,67ff.

Man Who Turned on The World, The, 67
Marine Biological Association, 39
Markov, Georgy, 110
McCarthy, Richard, 92
Medical Protection Against CBW, 99
Mighty Mite, 12,14
Mildenhall, 79ff.
mind control, 68
Mind Manipulators, The, 67
miosis, 22
mustard gas, 114

Nancekuke, 14,16,19,28ff.
  closure, 101
  open day, 97

napalm, 13
NASA, 69
Natural Environment Research Council, 39
nerve gas, 9,10,18ff.
neurotoxicity, 22
Newcastle, CIA in, 12,13
Northern Ireland, 112
Nottingham, Judith, 12,13

Official Secrets Act, 13,17,26,28, 30,34,41,97
Okinawa, 78,79
Ombudsman, 35
organophosphorus insecticides, 18,20,22
Otterburn, 55

patent, CBW 113,114
Patient's Association, 62
Perry Robinson, Dr. Julian, 24
petitions
　animal lovers, 94
　anti-CBW British, 7
　scientists, 12,93
plague, 60
Plague on Your Children, A, 9,12, 14,20
police weapons, 111
Porton under Public Health Laboratory Service, 107
protection of civilians, 59
psychochemicals, 9,10,67ff.
psychops, 112
Pugwash, 88ff.

quadripartite agreement, 92,100

research on CBW in US, 70ff.
ricin, 7,110
riot control techniques, 111
Rose, Professor Steven, 15
Rothschild, General, 11

Royal United Services Institute, 75
Russell, Bertrand, 87
Rydon, Professor, 11

sarin, 10,18,22,32
Schermuly, 13,15,55,76
science and politics, 106
Science, Technology and Society Association, 105
scientist's role in CBW, 107,108
seals, 39
scientists, training of, 101
secrecy, 9,113
secrets, 114
Seveso, 109
smallpox accident, 109,110
smoke, 45
soman, 18
sonic barrier, 40
space drugs, 69
Special Branch, 19
Spiegelberg, U, 20,24,33,35
Steel, David, 63,64
Stewart, Michael, 13
stockpiles of nerve gas, 19
storage of nerve gas, 38,78,79
STP, 10
Suffield, 72
surveillance, 93
Swedish attitude to CBW research, 9
Swedish International Peace Research Institute, 15,23,91

tabun, 10,18
teach-in on CBW, 8
tear gases, 10
telephone tapping, 93
tests in Panama, 71
TOCP, 31
training of scientists, 101
transport of chemical agents, 77

UK universities, CBW research in, 74,75
UN arms control, 103
UN on CBW, 85
USSR and verification, 104
Utah, sheep accident, 78

V agents, 10,19
verification of closure of plants, 41
Vietnam,
    disease in, 12
    protest against napalm and gas, 86
    war, 12
verification techniques, 104
volunteers, US army, 65

weather modification, 108
Whittaker, Dr Mary, 20,30
WHO, report on CBW, 19

Patrick Kinnersly
The Hazards of Work
A Worker's Guide to Health and Safety

The authoritative book on health and safety at work, with information on: physical hazards, patterns of work, chemical hazards, disease prevention, accidents, action, the legal machine, safety law, winning damages, industrial injury benefits, organising. It contains a directory of toxic substances.

'a detailed and well-documented handbook on virtually every aspect of industrial health and safety . . . essential reading . . .'
The Guardian

Lesley Doyal
with Imogen Pennell

The Political Economy of Health

Ill-health and disease are generally seen as misfortunes which just happen to people and which scientific medicine is on the point of eliminating or at least dedicated to combating.

In *The Political Economy of Health* the authors question these views in fundamental ways. They show that ill-health, in both the developed and underdeveloped world, is largely a product of the social and economic organisation of society. They show that medical practice and research are strongly influenced by their roles in maintaining a healthy labour force and in socialising and controlling people, and that the medical field provides a large and growing arena for the accumulation of capital.

Barbara Ehrenreich and Deirdre English
For Her Own Good
150 Years of the Experts' Advice to Women

For Her Own Good boldly reassesses 150 years of advice from the experts: gynaecologists and child psychologists, sociologists and psychoanalysts (including Freud), home economists and paediatricians (including Spock). Barbara Ehrenreich and Deirdre English show how the experts usurped women's age-old skills and then set themselves up as the sole authorities on everything from work to love. The onslaught of advice that followed has alway been justified as being *for her own good* – a service to women badly in need of guidance. In fact that 'scientific' guidance has again and again contained arrogant and unscientific judgements about women's body, mind and nature – as this book reveals in thorough and wryly humorous detail.

No longer willing to obey the experts quietly, women today are struggling to define their own identities. The authors offer a brilliant re-evaluation of the past and new perspectives on the future of the family, the cultural impact of science, and the meaning of 'liberation' in women's daily lives.

Barbara Ehrenreich and Deirdre English are the authors of two other classic studies of women and the experts: *Witches, Midwives and Nurses: A History of Women Healers* and *Complaints and Disorders: The Sexual Politics of Sickness*.

Dave Elliott
with Pat Coyne, Mike George and Roy Lewis
The Politics of Nuclear Power

In *The Politics of Nuclear Power*, Dave Elliott and his co-authors have written the first book on the subject to address itself to trade unionists as well as to people in the broader anti-nuclear movement. They consider the effects of the new industry on jobs, on trade union rights, on health and safety, and review critically the stated position of the trade union leaders.

They reveal who pays for the industry, and who benefits from it. They consider the evidence for alternative energy resources and show how we might avoid the traps of a nuclear-powered society.